OTHER BOOKS

Available on Amazon

Claim These Free Resources that Will Help You Unleash the Power of Your Words and Speak with Confidence. Visit **www.speakforsuccesshub.com/toolkit** for Access.

18 Free PDF Resources

30 Free Video Lessons

2 Free Workbooks

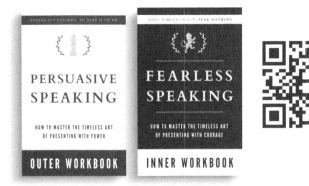

Claim These Free Resources that Will Help You Unleash the Power of Your Words and Speak with Confidence. Visit www.speakforsuccesshub.com/toolkit for Access.

18 Free PDF Resources

12 Iron Rules for Captivating Story, 21 Speeches that Changed the World, 341-Point Influence Checklist, 143 Persuasive Cognitive Biases, 17 Ways to Think On Your Feet, 18 Lies About Speaking Well, 137 Deadly Logical Fallacies, 12 Iron Rules For Captivating Slides, 371 Words that Persuade, 63 Truths of Speaking Well, 27 Laws of Empathy, 21 Secrets of Legendary Speeches, 19 Scripts that Persuade, 12 Iron Rules For Captivating Speech, 33 Laws of Charisma, 11 Influence Formulas, 219-Point Speech-Writing Checklist, 21 Eloquence Formulas

30 Free Video Lessons

We'll send you one free video lesson every day for 30 days, written and recorded by Peter D. Andrei. Days 1-10 cover authenticity, the prerequisite to confidence and persuasive power. Days 11-20 cover building self-belief and defeating communication anxiety. Days 21-30 cover how to speak with impact and influence, ensuring your words change minds instead of falling flat. Authenticity, self-belief, and impact – this course helps you master three components of confidence, turning even the most high-stakes presentations from obstacles into opportunities.

2 Free Workbooks

We'll send you two free workbooks, including long-lost excerpts by Dale Carnegie, the mega-bestselling author of *How to Win Friends and Influence People* (5,000,000 copies sold). *Fearless Speaking* guides you in the proven principles of mastering your inner game as a speaker. *Persuasive Speaking* guides you in the time-tested tactics of mastering your outer game by maximizing the power of your words. All of these resources complement the Speak for Success collection.

INFLUENCE

THE PSYCHOLOGY OF WORDS THAT
WIN HEARTS AND CHANGE MINDS

Peter Andrei

INFLUENCE

SPEAK FOR SUCCESS COLLECTION BOOK

IX

SPEAK
TRUTH
WELL
PRESS

A SUBSIDIARY OF SPEAK TRUTH WELL LLC
800 Boylston Street
Boston, MA 02199

SPEAK
TRUTH
WELL LLC

SPEAK FOR SUCCESS COLLECTION

Printed in the United States of America
40 39 38 37 36 35 34 33 32 31

While the author has made every effort to provide accurate internet addresses
at the time of publication, neither the publisher nor the author assumes any
responsibility for errors, or for changes that occur after publication. Further, the
publisher does not have any control over and does not assume any
responsibility for author or third-party websites or their content.

WHY DOES THIS HELP YOU?

I

The PDF resources cover topics like storytelling, logic, cognitive biases, empathy, charisma, and more. You can dig deeper into the specific topics that interest you most.

II

Many of the PDF resources are checklists, scripts, example-compilations, and formula-books. With these practical, step-by-step tools, you can quickly create messages that work.

III

With these free resources, you can supplement your reading of this book. You can find more specific guidance on the areas of communication you need to improve the most.

IV

The two workbooks offer practical and actionable guidance for speaking with complete confidence (*Fearless Speaking*) and irresistible persuasive power (*Persuasive Speaking*).

V

You can even learn from your phone with the free PDFs and the free video lessons, to develop your skills faster. The 30-lesson course reveals the secrets of building confidence.

VI

You are reading this because you want to improve your communication. These resources take you to the next level, helping you learn how to speak with power, impact, and confidence. We hope these resources make a difference. They are available here:

www.speakforsuccesshub.com/toolkit

From the desk of Peter Andrei
Speak Truth Well LLC
800 Boylston Street
Boston, MA 02199
pandreibusiness@gmail.com

May 15, 2021

What is Our Mission?

To whom it may concern:

The Wall Street Journal reports that public speaking is the world's biggest fear – bigger than being hit by a car. According to Columbia University, this pervasive, powerful, common phobia can reduce someone's salary by 10% or more. It can reduce someone's chances of graduating college by 10% and cut their chances of attaining a managerial or leadership position at work by 15%.

If weak presentation kills your good ideas, it kills your career. If weak communication turns every negotiation, meeting, pitch, speech, presentation, discussion, and interview into an obstacle (instead of an opportunity), it slows your progress. And if weak communication slows your progress, it tears a gaping hole in your confidence – which halts your progress.

Words can change the world. They can improve your station in life, lifting you forward and upward to higher and higher successes. But they have to be strong words spoken well: rarities in a world where most people fail to connect, engage, and persuade; fail to answer the question "why should we care about this?"; fail to impact, inspire, and influence; and, in doing so, fail to be all they could be.

Now zoom out. Multiply this dynamic by one thousand; one million; one billion. The individual struggle morphs into a problem for our communities, our countries, our world. Imagine the many millions of paradigm-shattering, life-changing, life-saving ideas that never saw the light of day. Imagine how many brilliant convictions were sunk in the shipyard. Imagine all that could have been that failed to be.

Speak Truth Well LLC solves this problem by teaching ambitious professionals how to turn communication from an obstacle into an engine: a tool for converting "what could be" into "what is." There is no upper limit: inexperienced speakers can become self-assured and impactful; veteran speakers can master the skill by learning advanced strategies; masters can learn how to outperform their former selves.

We achieve our mission by producing the best publications, articles, books, video courses, and coaching programs available on public speaking and communication, and at non-prohibitive prices. This combination of quality and accessibility has allowed Speak Truth Well to serve over 70,000 customers in its year of launch alone (2021). Grateful as we are, we hope to one day serve millions.

Dedicated to your success,

Peter Andrei
President of Speak Truth Well LLC
pandreibusiness@gmail.com

PROLOGUE:

This three-part prologue reveals my story, my work, and the practical and ethical principles of communication. It is not a mere introduction. It will help you get more out of the book. It is a preface to the entire 15-book Speak for Success collection. It will show you how to use the information with ease, confidence, and fluency, and how to get better results faster. If you would like to skip this, flip to page 50, or read only the parts of interest.

I

page XIII

MY STORY AND THE STORY OF THIS COLLECTION

how I discovered the hidden key to successful communication, public speaking, influence, and persuasion

II

page XXIV

THE 15-BOOK SPEAK FOR SUCCESS COLLECTION

confidence, leadership, charisma, influence, public speaking, eloquence, human nature, credibility - it's all here

III

page XXIX

THE PRACTICAL TACTICS AND ETHICAL PRINCIPLES

how to easily put complex strategies into action and how to use the power of words to improve the world

I

MY STORY AND THE STORY OF THIS COLLECTION

how I discovered the hidden key to successful communication, public speaking, influence, and persuasion (by reflecting on a painful failure)

HOW TO GAIN AN UNFAIR ADVANTAGE IN YOUR CAREER, BUSINESS, AND LIFE BY MASTERING THE POWER OF YOUR WORDS

I WAS SITTING IN MY OFFICE, TAPPING A PEN against my small wooden desk. My breaths were jagged, shallow, and rapid. My hands were shaking. I glanced at the clock: 11:31 PM. "I'm not ready." Have you ever had that thought?

I had to speak in front of 200 people the next morning. I had to convince them to put faith in my idea. But I was terrified, attacked by nameless, unreasoning, and unjustified terror which killed my ability to think straight, believe in myself, and get the job done.

Do you know the feeling?

After a sleepless night, the day came. I rose, wobbling on my tired legs. My head felt like it was filled with cotton candy. I couldn't direct my train of thoughts. A rushing waterfall of unhinged, self-destructive, and meaningless musings filled my head with an uncompromising cacophony of anxious, ricocheting nonsense.

"Call in sick."

"You're going to embarrass yourself."

"You're not ready."

I put on my favorite blue suit – my "lucky suit" – and my oversized blue-gold wristwatch; my "lucky" wristwatch.

"You're definitely not ready."

"That tie is ugly."

"You can't do this."

The rest went how you would expect. I drank coffee. Got in my car. Drove. Arrived. Waited. Waited. Waited. Spoke. Did poorly. Rushed back to my seat. Waited. Waited. Waited. Got in my car. Drove. Arrived home. Sat back in my wooden seat where I accurately predicted "I'm not ready" the night before.

Relieved it was over but disappointed with my performance, I placed a sheet of paper on the desk. I wrote "MY PROBLEMS" at the top, and under that, my prompt for the evening: "What did I do so badly? Why did everything feel so off? Why did the speech fail?"

"You stood in front of 200 people and looked at... a piece of paper, not unlike this one. What the hell were you thinking? You're not fooling anyone by reading a sentence and then looking up at them as you say it out loud. They know you're reading a manuscript, and they know what that means. You are unsure of yourself. You are unsure of your message. You are unprepared. Next: Why did you speak in that odd, low, monotone voice? That sounded like nails on a chalkboard. And it was inauthentic. Next: Why did you open by talking about yourself? Also, you're not particularly funny. No more jokes. And what was the structure of the speech? It had no structure. That, I feel, is probably a pretty big problem."

I believed in my idea, and I wanted to get it across. Of course, I wanted the tangible markers of a successful speech. I wanted action. I wanted the speech to change something in the real world. But my motivations were deeper than that. I wanted to see people "click" and come on board my way of thinking. I wanted to captivate the audience. I wanted to speak with an engaging, impactful voice, drawing the audience in, not repelling them. I wanted them to remember my message and to remember me. I wanted to feel, for just a moment, the thrill of power. But not the petty, forceful power of tyrants and dictators; the justified power – the earned power – of having a good idea and conveying it well; the power of Martin Luther King and John F. Kennedy; a power harnessed in service of a valuable idea, not the personal privilege of the speaker. And I wanted confidence: the quiet strength that comes from knowing your words don't stand in your way, but propel you and the ideas you care about to glorious new mountaintops.

Instead, I stood before the audience, essentially powerless. I spoke for 20 painful minutes – painful for them and for me – and then sat down. I barely made a dent in anyone's consciousness. I generated no excitement. Self-doubt draped its cold embrace over me. Anxiety built a wall between "what I am" and "what I could be."

I had tried so many different solutions. I read countless books on effective communication, asked countless effective communicators for their advice, and consumed countless courses on powerful public speaking. Nothing worked. All the "solutions" that didn't really solve my problem had one thing in common: they treated communication as an abstract art form. They were filled with vague, abstract pieces of advice like "think positive thoughts" and "be yourself." They confused me more than anything else. Instead of illuminating the secrets I had been looking for, they shrouded the elusive but indispensable skill of powerful speaking in uncertainty.

I knew I had to master communication. I knew that the world's most successful people are all great communicators. I knew that effective communication is the bridge between "what I have" and "what I want," or at least an essential part of that bridge. I knew that without effective communication – without the ability to influence, inspire, captivate, and move – I would be all but powerless.

I knew that the person who can speak up but doesn't is no better off than the person who can't speak at all. I heard a wise man say "If you can think and speak and write, you are absolutely deadly. Nothing can get in your way." I heard another wise man say "Speech is power: speech is to persuade, to convert, to compel. It is to bring another out of his bad sense into your good sense." I heard a renowned psychologist say "If you look at people who are remarkably successful across life, there's various reasons. But one of them is that they're unbelievably good at articulating what they're aiming at and strategizing and negotiating and enticing people with a vision forward. Get your words together... that makes you unstoppable. If you are an effective writer and speaker and communicator, you have all the authority and competence that there is."

When I worked in the Massachusetts State House for the Department of Public Safety and Homeland Security, I had the opportunity to speak with countless senators, state representatives, CEOs, and other successful people. In our conversations, however brief, I always asked the same question: "What are the ingredients of your success? What got you where you are?" 100% of them said effective communication. There was not one who said anything else. No matter their field – whether they were entrepreneurs, FBI agents, political leaders, business leaders, or multimillionaire donors – they all pointed to one skill: the ability to convey powerful words in powerful ways. Zero exceptions.

Can you believe it? It still astonishes me.

My problem, and I bet this may be your obstacle as well, was that most of the advice I consumed on this critical skill barely scratched the surface. Sure, it didn't make matters worse, and it certainly offered some improvement, but only in inches when I needed progress in miles. If I stuck with the mainstream public speaking advice, I knew I wouldn't unleash the power of my words. And if I didn't do that, I knew I would always accomplish much less than I could. I knew I would suffocate my own potential. I knew I would feel a rush of crippling anxiety every time I was asked to give a presentation. I knew I would live a life of less fulfillment, less success, less achievement, more frustration, more difficulty, and more anxiety. I knew my words would never become all they could be, which means that I would never become all I could be.

To make matters worse, the mainstream advice – which is not wrong, but simply not deep enough – is everywhere. Almost every article, book, or course published on this subject falls into the mainstream category. And to make matters worse, it's almost impossible to know that until you've spent your hard-earned money and scarce time with the resource. And even then, you might just shrug, and assume that shallow, abstract advice is all there is to the "art" of public speaking. As far as I'm concerned, this is a travesty.

I kept writing. "It felt like there was no real motive; no real impulse to action. Why did they need to act? You didn't tell them. What would happen if they didn't? You didn't tell them that either. Also, you tried too hard to put on a formal façade; you spoke in strange, twisted ways. It didn't sound sophisticated. And your mental game was totally off. You let your mind fill with destructive, doubtful, self-defeating thoughts. And your preparation was totally backward. It did more to set bad habits in stone than it did to set you up for success. And you tried to build suspense at one point but revealed the final point way too early, ruining the effect."

I went on and on until I had a stack of papers filled with problems. "That's no good," I thought. I needed solutions. Everything else I tried failed. But I had one more idea: "I remember reading a great speech. What was it? Oh yeah, that's right: JFK's inaugural address. Let me go pull it up and see why it was so powerful." And that's when everything changed.

I grabbed another sheet of paper. I opened JFK's inaugural address on my laptop. I started reading. Observing. Analyzing.

Reverse-engineering. I started writing down what I saw. Why did it work? Why was it powerful? I was like an archaeologist, digging through his speech for the secrets of powerful communication. I got more and more excited as I kept going. It was late at night, but the shocking and invaluable discoveries I was making gave me a burst of energy. It felt like JFK – one of the most powerful and effective speakers of all time – was coaching me in his rhetorical secrets, showing me how to influence an audience, draw them into my narrative, and find words that get results.

"Oh, so that's how you grab attention."

"Aha! So, if I tell them this, they will see why it matters."

"Fascinating – I can apply this same structure to my speech."

Around 3:00 in the morning, an epiphany hit me like a ton of bricks. That night, a new paradigm was born. A new opportunity emerged for all those who want to unleash the unstoppable power of their words. This new opportunity changed everything for me and eventually, tens of thousands of others. It is now my mission to bring it to millions, so that good people know what they need to know to use their words to achieve their dreams and improve the world.

Want to hear the epiphany?

The mainstream approach: Communication is an art form. It is unlike those dry, boring, "academic" subjects. There are no formulas. There are no patterns. It's all about thinking positive thoughts, faking confidence, and making eye contact. Some people are naturally gifted speakers. For others, the highest skill level they can attain is "not horrible."

The consequences of the mainstream approach: Advice that barely scratches the surface of the power of words. Advice that touches only the tip of the tip of the iceberg. A limited body of knowledge that blinds itself to thousands of hidden, little-known communication strategies that carry immense power; that blinds itself to 95% of what great communication really is. Self-limiting dogmas about who can do what, and how great communicators become great. Half the progress in twice the time, and everything that entails: missed opportunities, unnecessary and preventable frustration and anxiety, and confusion about what to say and how to say it. How do I know? Because I've been there. It's not pretty.

My epiphany, the new Speak for Success paradigm: Communication is as much a science as it is an art. You can study words that changed the world, uncover the hidden secrets of their power, and apply these proven principles to your own message. You can discover precisely what made great communicators great and adopt the same strategies. You can do this without being untrue to yourself or flatly imitating others. In fact, you can do this while being truer to yourself and more original than you ever have been before. Communication is not unpredictable, wishy-washy, or abstract. You can apply predictable processes and principles to reach your goals and get results. You can pick and choose from thousands of little-known speaking strategies, combining your favorite to create a unique communication approach that suits you perfectly. You can effortlessly use the same tactics of the world's most transformational leaders and speakers, and do so automatically, by default, without even thinking about it, as a matter of effortless habit. That's power.

The benefits of the Speak for Success paradigm: Less confusion. More confidence. Less frustration. More clarity. Less anxiety. More courage. You understand the whole iceberg of effective communication. As a result, your words captivate others. You draw them into a persuasive narrative, effortlessly linking your desires and their motives. You know exactly what to say. You know exactly how to say it. You know exactly how to keep your head clear; you are a master of the mental game. Your words can move mountains. Your words are the most powerful tools in your arsenal, and you use them to seize opportunities, move your mission forward, and make the world a better place. Simply put, you speak for success.

Fast forward a few years.

I was sitting in my office at my small wooden desk. My breaths were deep, slow, and steady. My entire being – mind, body, soul – was poised and focused. I set my speech manuscript to the side. I glanced at the clock: 12:01 AM. "Let's go. I'm ready."

I had to speak in front of 200 people the next morning. I had to convince them to put faith in my idea. And I was thrilled, filled with genuine gratitude at the opportunity to do what I love: get up in front of a crowd, think clearly, speak well, and get the job done.

I slept deeply. I dreamt vividly. I saw myself giving the speech. I saw myself victorious, in every sense of the word. I heard applause. I saw their facial expressions. I rose. My head was clear. My mental game was pristine. My mind was an ally, not an obstacle.

"This is going to be fun."

"I'll do my best, and whatever happens, happens."

"I'm so lucky that I get to do this again."

I put on my lucky outfit: the blue suit and the blue-gold watch.

"Remember the principles. They work."

"You developed a great plan last night. It's a winner."

"I can't wait."

The rest went how you would expect. I ate breakfast. Got in my car. Drove. Arrived. Waited. Waited. Waited. Spoke. Succeeded. Walked back to my seat. Waited. Waited. Waited. Got in my car. Drove. Arrived home. Sat back in my wooden seat where I accurately predicted "I'm ready" the night before.

I got my idea across perfectly. My message succeeded: it motivated action and created real-world change. I saw people "click" when I hit the rhetorical peak of my speech. I saw them leaning forward, totally hushed, completely absorbed. I applied the proven principles of engaging and impactful vocal modulation. I knew they would remember me and my message; I engineered my words to be memorable. I felt the thrilling power of giving a great speech. I felt the quiet confidence of knowing that my words carried weight; that they could win hearts, change minds, and help me reach the heights of my potential. I tore off the cold embrace of self-doubt. I defeated communication anxiety and broke down the wall between "what I am" and "what I could be."

Disappointed it was over but pleased with my performance, I placed a sheet of paper on the desk. I wrote "Speak Truth Well" and started planning what would become my business.

To date, we have helped tens of thousands of people gain an unfair advantage in their career, business, and life by unleashing the power of their words. And they experienced the exact same transformation I experienced when they applied the system.

If you tried to master communication before but haven't gotten the results you wanted, it's because of the mainstream approach; an approach that tells you "smiling at the audience" and "making eye contact" is all you need to know to speak well. That's not exactly a malicious lie – they don't know any better – but it is completely incorrect and severely harmful.

If you've been concerned that you won't be able to become a vastly more effective and confident communicator, I want to put those fears to rest. I felt the same way. The people I work with felt the same way. We just needed the right system. One public speaking book written by the director of a popular public speaking forum – I won't name names – wants you to believe that there are "nine public speaking secrets of the world's top minds." Wrong: There are many more than nine. If you feel that anyone who would boil down communication to just nine secrets is either missing something or holding it back, you're right. And the alternative is a much more comprehensive and powerful system. It's a system that gave me and everyone I worked with the transformation we were looking for.

Want to Talk? Email Me:

PANDREIBUSINESS@GMAIL.COM

This is My Personal Email.
I Read Every Message and
Respond in Under 12 Hours.

Visit Our Digital Headquarters:

WWW.SPEAKFORSUCCESSHUB.COM

See All Our Free Resources, Books, Courses, and Services.

THE 15-BOOK SPEAK FOR SUCCESS COLLECTION

confidence, leadership, charisma, influence, public speaking, eloquence, human nature, credibility – it's all here, in a unified collection

MASTER EVERY ASPECT OF COMMUNICATION

T HE BESTSELLING SPEAK FOR SUCCESS COLLECTION covers every aspect of communication. Each book in the collection includes diagrams that visualize the essential principles, chapter summaries that remind you of the main ideas, and checklists of the action items in each section, all designed to help you consult the set as a reference.

This series is a cohesive, comprehensive set. After writing the first book, I realized how much information I couldn't fit into it. I wrote the second. After writing the second, the same thing happened. I wrote the third. The pattern continued. As of this writing, there are fifteen books in the collection. After writing each book, I felt called to write another. It is the ultimate communication encyclopedia.

Aside from a small amount of necessary overlap on the basics, each book is a distinct unit that focuses on an entirely new set of principles, strategies, and communication secrets. For example, *Eloquence* reveals the secrets of language that sounds good; *Trust is Power* reveals the secrets of speaking with credibility; *Public Speaking Mastery* reveals a blueprint for delivering speeches.

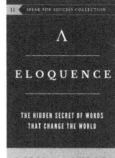

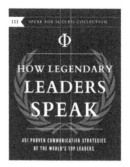

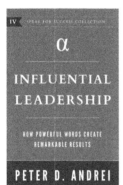

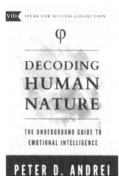

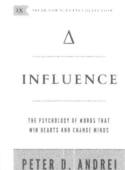

"The most complete and comprehensive collection of communication wisdom ever compiled." – Amazon Customer

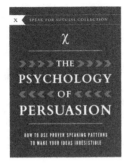

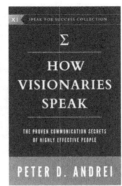

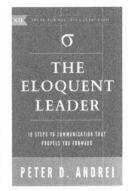

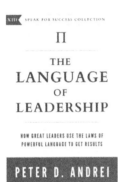

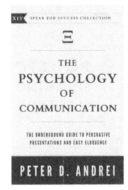

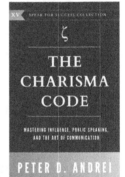

"I love the diagrams and summary checklists. I have all 15 on my shelf, and regularly refer back to them." – Amazon Customer

You Can Learn More Here:
www.speakforsuccesshub.com/series

...................................A Brief Overview...................................

- I wrote *How Highly Effective People Speak* to reveal the hidden patterns in the words of the world's most successful and powerful communicators, so that you can adopt the same tactics and speak with the same impact and influence.

- I wrote *Eloquence* to uncover the formulas of beautiful, moving, captivating, and powerful words, so that you can use these exact same step-by-step structures to quickly make your language electrifying, charismatic, and eloquent.

- I wrote *How Legendary Leaders Speak* to illuminate the little-known five-step communication process the top leaders of the past 500 years all used to spread their message, so that you can use it to empower your ideas and get results.

- I wrote *Influential Leadership* to expose the differences between force and power and to show how great leaders use the secrets of irresistible influence to develop gentle power, so that you can move forward and lead with ease.

- I wrote *Public Speaking Mastery* to shatter the myths and expose the harmful advice about public speaking, and to offer a proven, step-by-step framework for speaking well, so that you can always speak with certainty and confidence.

- I wrote *The 7 Keys to Confidence* to bring to light the ancient 4,000-year-old secrets I used to master the mental game and speak in front of hundreds without a second of self-doubt or anxiety, so that you can feel the same freedom.

- I wrote *Trust is Power* to divulge how popular leaders and career communicators earn our trust, speak with credibility, and use this to rise to new heights of power, so that you can do the same thing to advance your purpose and mission.

- I wrote *Decoding Human Nature* to answer the critical question "what do people want?" and reveal how to use this knowledge to develop unparalleled influence, so that people adopt your idea, agree with your position, and support you.

- I wrote *Influence* to unearth another little-known five-step process for winning hearts and changing minds, so that you can know with certainty that your message will persuade people, draw support, and motivate enthusiastic action.

- I wrote *The Psychology of Persuasion* to completely and fully unveil everything about the psychology behind "Yes, I love it! What's the next step?" so that you can use easy step-by-step speaking formulas that get people to say exactly that.

- I wrote *How Visionaries Speak* to debunk common lies about effective communication that hold you back and weaken your words, so that you can boldly share your ideas without accidentally sabotaging your own message.

- I wrote *The Eloquent Leader* to disclose the ten steps to communicating with power and persuasion, so that you don't miss any of the steps and fail to connect, captivate, influence, and inspire in a crucial high-stakes moment.

- I wrote *The Language of Leadership* to unpack the unique, hidden-in-plain-sight secrets of how presidents and world-leaders build movements with the laws of powerful language, so that you use them to propel yourself forward.

- I wrote *The Psychology of Communication* to break the news that most presentations succeed or fail in the first thirty seconds and to reveal proven, step-by-step formulas that grab, hold, and direct attention, so that yours succeeds.

- I wrote *The Charisma Code* to shatter the myths and lies about charisma and reveal its nature as a concrete skill you can master with proven strategies, so that people remember you, your message, and how you electrified the room.

- **Learn more: www.speakforsuccesshub.com/series**

III

PRACTICAL TACTICS AND ETHICAL PRINCIPLES

how to easily put complex strategies into action and how to use the power of words to improve the world in an ethical and effective way

MOST COMMUNICATION BOOKS

HAVE YOU READ ANOTHER BOOK ON COMMUNICATION? If you have, let me remind you what you probably learned. And if you haven't, let me briefly spoil 95% of them. "Prepare. Smile. Dress to impress. Keep it simple. Overcome your fears. Speak from the heart. Be authentic. Show them why you care. Speak in terms of their interests. To defeat anxiety, know your stuff. Emotion persuades, not logic. Speak with confidence. Truth sells. And respect is returned."

There you have it. That is most of what you learn in most communication books. None of it is wrong. None of it is misleading. Those ideas are true and valuable. But they are not enough. They are only the absolute basics. And my job is to offer you much more.

Einstein said that "if you can't explain it in a sentence, you don't know it well enough." He also told us to "make it as simple as possible, but no simpler." You, as a communicator, must satisfy both of these maxims, one warning against the dangers of excess complexity, and one warning against the dangers of excess simplicity.

And I, as someone who communicates about communication in my books, courses, and coaching, must do the same.

THE SPEAK FOR SUCCESS SYSTEM

The Speak for Success system makes communication as simple as possible. Other communication paradigms make it even simpler. Naturally, this means our system is more complex. This is an unavoidable consequence of treating communication as a deep and concrete science instead of a shallow and abstract art. If you don't dive into learning communication at all, you miss out. I'm sure you agree with that. But if you don't dive *deep*, you still miss out.

THE FOUR QUADRANTS OF COMMUNICATION

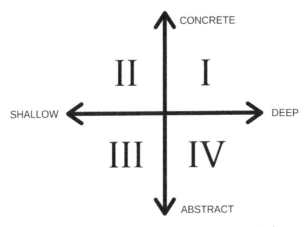

FIGURE VIII: There are four predominant views of communication (whether it takes the form of public speaking, negotiation, writing, or debating is irrelevant). The first view is that communication is concrete and deep. The second view is that communication is concrete and shallow. The third view is that communication is shallow and abstract. The fourth view is that communication is deep and abstract.

WHAT IS COMMUNICATION?

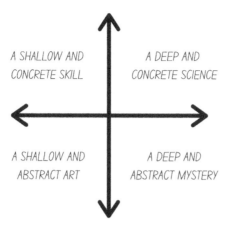

FIGURE VII: The first view treats communication as a science: "There are concrete formulas, rules, principles, and strategies, and they go very deep." The second view treats it as a skill: "Yes, there are concrete formulas, rules, and strategies, but they don't go very deep." The third view treats it as an art: "Rules? Formulas? It's not that complicated. Just smile and think positive thoughts." The fourth view treats it as a mystery: "How are some people such effective communicators? I will never know…"

WHERE WE STAND ON THE QUESTION

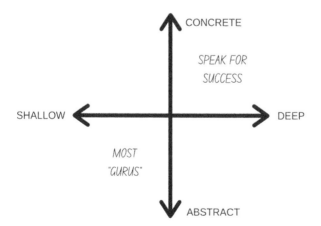

FIGURE VI: Speak for Success takes the view that communication is a deep and concrete science. (And by

"takes the view," I mean "has discovered.") Most other
communication writers, thought-leaders, public speaking
coaches, and individuals and organizations in this niche
treat communication as a shallow and abstract art.

This doesn't mean the Speak for Success system neglects the basics. It only means it goes far beyond the basics, and that it doesn't turn simple ideas into 200 pages of filler. It also doesn't mean that the Speak for Success system is unnecessarily complex. It is as simple as it can possibly be.

In this book, and in the other books of the Speak for Success collection, you'll find simple pieces of advice, easy formulas, and straightforward rules. You'll find theories, strategies, tactics, mental models, and principles. None of this should pose a challenge. But you'll also find advanced and complicated strategies. These might.

What is the purpose of the guide on the top of the next page? To reveal the methods that make advanced strategies easy. When you use the tactics revealed in this guide, the difficulty of using the advanced strategies drops dramatically. They empower you to use complicated and unfamiliar persuasive strategies with ease. If the 15-book Speak for Success collection is a complete encyclopedia of communication, to be used like a handbook, then this guide is a handbook for the handbook.

A SAMPLING OF EASY AND HARD STRATEGIES

Easy and Simple	Hard and Complicated
Use Four-Corner Eye Contact	The Fluency-Magnitude Matrix
Appeal to Their Values	The VPB Triad
Describe the Problem You Solve	The Illusory Truth Effect
Use Open Body Language	Percussive Rhythm
Tell a Quick Story	Alliterative Flow
Appeal to Emotion	Stacking and Layering Structures
Project Your Voice	The Declaratory Cascade
Keep it as Simple as Possible	Alternating Semantic Sentiments

THE PRACTICAL TACTICS

RECOGNIZE THAT, WITH PRACTICE, YOU can use any strategy extemporaneously. Some people can instantly use even the most complex strategies in the Speak for Success collection after reading them just once. They are usually experienced communicators, often with competitive experience. This is not an expectation, but a possibility, and with practice, a probability.

CREATE A COMMUNICATION PLAN. Professional communication often follows a strategic plan. Put these techniques into your plan. Following an effective plan is not harder than following an ineffective one. Marshall your arguments. Marshall your rhetoric. Stack the deck. Know what you know, and how to say it.

DESIGN AN MVP. If you are speaking on short notice, you can create a "minimum viable plan." This can be a few sentences on a notecard jotted down five minutes before speaking. The same principle of formal communication plans applies: While advanced strategies may overburden you if you attempt them in an impromptu setting, putting them into a plan makes them easy.

MASTER YOUR RHETORICAL STACK. Master one difficult strategy. Master another one. Combine them. Master a third. Build out a "rhetorical stack" of ten strategies you can use fluently, in impromptu or extemporaneous communication. Pick strategies that come fluently to you and that complement each other.

PRACTICE THEM TO FLUENCY. I coach a client who approached me and said he wants to master every strategy I ever compiled. That's a lot. As of this writing, we're 90 one-hour sessions in. To warm up for one of our sessions, I gave him a challenge: "Give an impromptu speech on the state of the American economy, and after you stumble, hesitate, or falter four times, I'll cut you off. The challenge is to see how long you can go." He spoke for 20 minutes without a single mistake. After 20 minutes, he brought the impromptu speech to a perfect, persuasive, forceful, and eloquent conclusion. And he naturally and fluently used advanced strategies throughout his impromptu speech. After he closed the speech (which he did because he wanted to get on with the session), I asked him if he thought deeply about the strategies he used. He said no. He used them thoughtlessly. Why? Because he practiced them. You can too. You can practice them on your own. You don't need an audience. You don't need a coach. You don't even need to speak. Practice in your head. Practice ones that resonate with you. Practice with topics you care about.

KNOW TEN TIMES MORE THAN YOU INTEND TO SAY. And know what you do intend to say about ten times more fluently than you need to. This gives your mind room to relax, and frees up cognitive bandwidth to devote to strategy and rhetoric in real-time. Need to speak for five minutes? Be able to speak for 50. Need to read it three times to be able to deliver it smoothly? Read it 30 times.

INCORPORATE THEM IN SLIDES. You can use your slides or visual aids to help you ace complicated strategies. If you can't remember the five steps of a strategy, your slides can still follow them. Good slides aren't harder to use than bad slides.

USE THEM IN WRITTEN COMMUNICATION. You can read your speech. In some situations, this is more appropriate than impromptu or extemporaneous speaking. And if a strategy is difficult to remember in impromptu speaking, you can write it into your speech. And let's not forget about websites, emails, letters, etc.

PICK AND CHOOSE EASY ONES. Use strategies that come naturally and don't overload your mind. Those that do are counterproductive in fast-paced situations.

TAKE SMALL STEPS TO MASTERY. Practice one strategy. Practice it again. Keep going until you master it. Little by little, add to your base of strategies. But never take steps that overwhelm you. Pick a tactic. Practice it. Master it. Repeat.

MEMORIZE AN ENTIRE MESSAGE. Sometimes this is the right move. Is it a high-stakes message? Do you have the time? Do you have the energy? Given the situation, would a memorized delivery beat an impromptu, in-the-moment, spontaneous delivery? If you opt for memorizing, using advanced strategies is easy.

USE ONE AT A TIME. Pick an advanced strategy. Deliver it. Now what? Pick another advanced strategy. Deliver it. Now another. Have you been speaking for a while? Want to bring it to a close? Pick a closing strategy. For some people, using advanced strategies extemporaneously is easy, but only if they focus on one at a time.

MEMORIZE A KEY PHRASE. Deliver your impromptu message as planned, but add a few short, memorized key phrases throughout that include advanced strategies.

CREATE TALKING POINTS. Speak from a list of pre-written bullet-points; big-picture ideas you seek to convey. This is halfway between fully impromptu speaking and using a script. It's not harder to speak from a strategic and persuasively-advanced list of talking points than it is to speak from a persuasively weak list. You can either memorize your talking points, or have them in front of you as a guide.

TREAT IT LIKE A SCIENCE. At some point, you struggled with a skill that you now perform effortlessly. You mastered it. It's a habit. You do it easily, fluently, and thoughtlessly. You can do it while you daydream. Communication is the same. These tactics, methods, and strategies are not supposed to be stuck in the back of your mind as you speak. They are supposed to be ingrained in your habits.

RELY ON FLOW. In fast-paced and high-stakes situations, you usually don't plan every word, sentence, and idea consciously and deliberately. Rather, you let your subconscious mind take over. You speak from a flow state. In flow, you may flawlessly execute strategies that would have overwhelmed your conscious mind.

LISTEN TO THE PROMPTS. You read a strategy and found it difficult to use extemporaneously. But as you speak, your subconscious mind gives you a prompt:

"this strategy would work great here." Your subconscious mind saw the opportunity and surfaced the prompt. You execute it, and you do so fluently and effortlessly.

FOLLOW THE FIVE-STEP CYCLE. First, find truth. Research. Prepare. Learn. Second, define your message. Figure out what you believe about what you learned. Third, polish your message with rhetorical strategies, without distorting the precision with which it conveys the truth. Fourth, practice the polished ideas. Fifth, deliver them. The endeavor of finding truth comes before the rhetorical endeavor. First, find the right message. Then, find the best way to convey it.

CREATE YOUR OWN STRATEGY. As you learn new theories, mental models, and principles of psychology and communication, you may think of a new strategy built around the theories, models, and principles. Practice it, test it, and codify it.

STACK GOOD HABITS. An effective communicator is the product of his habits. If you want to be an effective communicator, stack good communication habits (and break bad ones). This is a gradual process. It doesn't happen overnight.

DON'T TRY TO USE THEM. Don't force it. If a strategy seems too difficult, don't try to use it. You might find yourself using it anyway when the time is right.

KNOW ONLY ONE. If you master one compelling communication strategy, like one of the many powerful three-part structures that map out a persuasive speech, that can often be enough to drastically and dramatically improve your impact.

REMEMBER THE SHORTCOMING OF MODELS. All models are wrong, but some are useful. Many of these complex strategies and theories are models. They represent reality, but they are not reality. They help you navigate the territory, but they are not the territory. They are a map, to be used if it helps you navigate, and to be discarded the moment it prevents you from navigating.

DON'T LET THEM INHIBIT YOU. Language flows from thought. You've got to have something to say. And *then* you make it as compelling as possible. And *then* you shape it into something poised and precise; persuasive and powerful; compelling and convincing. Meaning and message come first. Rhetoric comes second. Don't take all this discussion of "advanced communication strategies," "complex communication tactics," and "the deep and concrete science of communication" to suggest that the basics don't matter. They do. Tell the truth as precisely and boldly as you can. Know your subject-matter like the back of your hand. Clear your mind and focus on precisely articulating exactly what you believe to be true. Be authentic. The advanced strategies are not supposed to stand between you and your audience. They are not supposed to stand between you and your authentic and spontaneous self – they are supposed to be integrated with it. They are not an end in themselves, but a means to the end of persuading the maximum number of people to adopt truth. Trust your instinct. Trust your intuition. It won't fail you.

MASTERING ONE COMMUNICATION SKILL

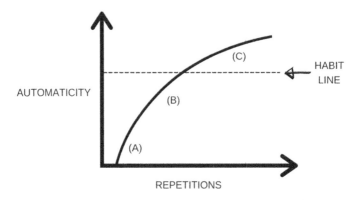

FIGURE V: Automaticity is the extent to which you do something automatically, without thinking about it. At the start of building a communication habit, it has low automaticity. You need to think about it consciously (A). After more repetitions, it gets easier and more automatic (B). Eventually, the behavior becomes more automatic than deliberate. At this point, it becomes a habit (C).

MASTERING COMMUNICATION

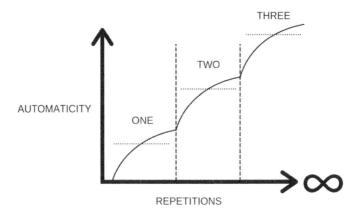

FIGURE IV: Layer good communication habits on top of each other. Go through the learning curve over and over again. When you master the first good habit, jump to the second. This pattern will take you to mastery.

THE FOUR LEVELS OF KNOWING

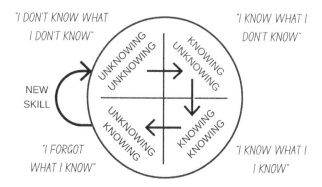

FIGURE III: First, you don't know you don't know it. Then, you discover it and know you don't know it. Then, you practice it and know you know it. Then, it becomes a habit. You forget you know it. It's ingrained in your habits.

REVISITING THE LEARNING CURVE

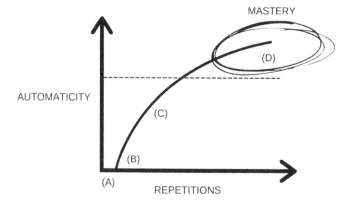

FIGURE II: Note the stages of knowing on the learning curve: unknowing unknowing (A), knowing unknowing (B), knowing knowing (C), unknowing knowing (D).

WHAT'S REALLY HAPPENING?

Have you ever thought deeply about what happens when you communicate? Let's run through the mile-high view.

At some point in your life, you bumped into an experience. You observed. You learned. The experience changed you. Your neural networks connected in new ways. New rivers of neurons began to flow through them.

The experience etched a pattern into your neurobiology representing information about the moral landscape of the universe; a map of *where we are, where we should go, and how we should make the journey.* This is meaning. This is your message.

Now, you take the floor before a crowd. Whether you realize it or not, you want to copy the neural pattern from your mind to their minds. You want to show them where we are, where we should go, and how we should make the journey.

So, you speak. You gesture. You intone. Your words convey meaning. Your body language conveys meaning. Your voice conveys meaning. You flood them with a thousand different inputs, some as subtle as the contraction of a single facial muscle, some as obvious as your opening line. Your character, your intentions, and your goals seep into your speech. Everyone can see them. Everyone can see you.

Let's step into the mind of one of your audience members. Based on all of this, based on a thousand different inputs, based on complex interactions between their conscious and nonconscious minds, the ghost in the machine steps in, and by a dint of free will, acts as the final arbiter and makes a choice. A mind is changed. You changed it. And changing it changed you. You became more confident, more articulate, and deeper; more capable, more impactful, and stronger.

Communication is connection. One mind, with a consciousness at its base, seeks to use ink or pixels or airwaves to connect to another. Through this connection, it seeks to copy neural patterns about the present, the future, and the moral landscape. Whatever your message is, the underlying connection is identical. How could it not be?

IS IT ETHICAL?

By "it," I mean deliberately using language to get someone to do or think something. Let's call this rhetoric. We could just as well call it persuasion, influence, communication, or even leadership itself.

The answer is yes. The answer is no. Rhetoric is a helping hand. It is an iron fist. It is Martin Luther King's dream. It is Stalin's nightmare. It is the "shining city on the hill." It is the iron curtain. It is "the pursuit of happiness." It is the trail of tears. It is "liberty, equality, and brotherhood." It is the reign of terror. Rhetoric is a tool. It is neither good nor evil. It is a reflection of our nature.

Rhetoric can motivate love, peace, charity, strength, patience, progress, prosperity, common sense, common purpose, courage, hope, generosity, and unity. It can also sow the seeds of division, fan the flames of tribalism, and beat back the better angels of our nature.

Rhetoric is the best of us and the worst of us. It is as good as you are. It is as evil as you are. It is as peace-loving as you are. It is as hate-mongering as you are. And I know what you are. I know my readers are generous, hardworking people who want to build a better future for themselves, for their families, and for all humankind. I know that if you have these tools in your hands, you will use them to achieve a moral mission. That's why putting them in your hands is my mission.

Joseph Chatfield said "[rhetoric] is the power to talk people out of their sober and natural opinions." I agree. But it is also the power to talk people out of their wrong and harmful opinions. And if you're using rhetoric to talk people out of their sober opinions, the problem isn't rhetoric, it's you.

In the *Institutes of Rhetoric*, Roman rhetorician Quintilian wrote the following: "The orator then, whom I am concerned to form, shall be the orator as defined by Marcus Cato, a good man, skilled in speaking. But above all he must possess the quality which Cato places first and which is in the very nature of things the greatest and most important, that is, he must be a good man. This is essential not merely on account of the fact that, if the powers of eloquence serve only to lend arms to crime, there can be nothing more pernicious than eloquence to public and private welfare alike, while I myself, who have labored to the best of my ability to contribute something of the value to oratory, shall have rendered the worst of services to mankind, if I forge these weapons not for a soldier, but for a robber."

Saint Augustine, who was trained in the classical schools of rhetoric in the 3rd century, summed it up well: "Rhetoric, after all, being the art of persuading people to accept something, whether it is true or false, would anyone dare to maintain that truth should stand there without any weapons in the hands of its defenders against falsehood; that those speakers, that is to say, who are trying to convince their hearers of what is untrue, should know how to get them on their side, to gain their attention and have them eating out of their hands by their opening remarks, while these who are defending the truth should not? That those should utter their lies briefly, clearly, plausibly, and these should state their truths in a manner too boring to listen to, too obscure to understand, and finally too repellent to believe? That those should attack the truth with specious arguments, and assert falsehoods, while these should be incapable of either defending the truth or refuting falsehood? That those, to move and force the minds of their hearers into error, should be able by their style to terrify them, move them to tears, make them laugh, give them rousing encouragement, while these on behalf of truth stumble along slow, cold and half asleep?"

THE ETHICS OF PERSUASION

REFER BACK TO THIS ETHICAL GUIDE as needed. I created this in a spirit of humility, for my benefit as much as for the benefit of my readers. And you don't have to choose between efficacy and ethics. When I followed these principles, my words became more ethical *and* more powerful.

FOLLOW THESE TWELVE RULES. Do not use false, fabricated, misrepresented, distorted, or irrelevant evidence to support claims. Do not intentionally use specious, unsupported, or illogical reasoning. Do not represent yourself as informed or as an "expert" on a subject when you are not. Do not use irrelevant appeals to divert attention from the issue at hand. Do not cause intense but unreflective emotional reactions. Do not link your idea to emotion-laden values, motives, or goals to which it is not related. Do not hide your real purpose or self-interest, the group you represent, or your position as an advocate of a viewpoint. Do not distort, hide, or misrepresent the number, scope, or intensity of bad effects. Do not use emotional appeals that lack a basis of evidence or reasoning or that would fail if the audience examined the subject themselves. Do not oversimplify complex, gradation-laden situations into simplistic two-valued, either/or, polar views or choices. Do not pretend certainty where tentativeness and degrees of probability would be more accurate. Do not advocate something you do not believe (Johannesen et al., 2021).

APPLY THIS GOLDEN HEURISTIC. In a 500,000-word book, you might be able to tell your audience everything you know about a subject. In a five-minute persuasive speech, you can only select a small sampling of your knowledge. Would learning your entire body of knowledge result in a significantly different reaction than hearing the small sampling you selected? If the answer is yes, that's a problem.

SWING WITH THE GOOD EDGE. Rhetoric is a double-edged sword. It can express good ideas well. It can also express bad ideas well. Rhetoric makes ideas attractive; tempting; credible; persuasive. Don't use it to turn weakly-worded lies into well-worded lies. Use it to turn weakly-worded truths into well-worded truths.

TREAT TRUTH AS THE HIGHEST GOOD. Use any persuasive strategy, unless using it in your circumstances would distort the truth. The strategies should not come between you and truth, or compromise your honesty and authenticity.

AVOID THE SPIRIT OF DECEIT. Wrong statements are incorrect statements you genuinely believe. Lies are statements you know are wrong but convey anyway. Deceitful statements are not literally wrong, but you convey them with the intent to mislead, obscure, hide, or manipulate. Hiding relevant information is not literally lying (saying you conveyed all the information would be). Cherry-picking facts is not literally lying (saying there are no other facts would be). Using clever innuendo to twist reality without making any concrete claims is not literally lying (knowingly making a false accusation would be). And yet, these are all examples of deceit.

ONLY USE STRATEGIES IF THEY ARE ACCURATE. Motivate unified thinking. Inspire loving thinking. These strategies sound good. Use the victim-perpetrator-benevolence structure. Paint a common enemy. Appeal to tribal psychology. These strategies sound bad. But when reality lines up with the strategies that sound bad, they become good. They are only bad when they are inaccurate or move people down a bad path. *But the same is true for the ones that sound good.* Should Winston Churchill have motivated unified thinking? Not toward his enemy. Should he have avoided appealing to tribal psychology to strengthen the Allied war effort? Should he have avoided painting a common enemy? Should he have avoided portraying the victimization of true victims and the perpetration of a true perpetrator? Should he have avoided calling people to act as the benevolent force for good, protecting the victim and beating back the perpetrator? Don't use the victim-perpetrator-benevolence structure if there aren't clear victims and perpetrators. This is demagoguery. Painting false victims disempowers them. But if there are true victims and perpetrators, stand up for the victims and stand against the perpetrators, calling others to join you as a benevolent force for justice. Don't motivate unified thinking when standing against evil. Don't hold back from portraying a common enemy when there is one. Some strategies might sound morally suspect. Some might sound inherently good. But it depends on the situation. Every time I say "do X to achieve Y," remember the condition: "if it is accurate and moves people up a good path."

APPLY THE TARES TEST: truthfulness of message, authenticity of persuader, respect for audience, equity of persuasive appeal, and social impact (TARES).

REMEMBER THE THREE-PART VENN DIAGRAM: words that are authentic, effective, and true. Donald Miller once said "I'm the kind of person who wants to present my most honest, authentic self to the world, so I hide backstage and rehearse honest and authentic lines until the curtain opens." There's nothing dishonest or inauthentic about choosing your words carefully and making them more effective, as long as they remain just as true. Rhetoric takes a messy marble brick of truth and sculpts it into a poised, precise, and perfect statue. It takes weak truths and makes them strong. Unfortunately, it can do the same for weak lies. But preparing, strategizing, and sculpting is not inauthentic. Unskillfulness is no more authentic than skillfulness. Unpreparedness is no more authentic than preparedness.

APPLY FITZPATRICK AND GAUTHIER'S THREE-QUESTION ANALYSIS. For what purpose is persuasion being employed? Toward what choices and with what consequences for individual lives is it being used? Does the persuasion contribute to or interfere with the audience's decision-making process (Lumen, 2016)?

STRENGTHEN THE TRUTH. Rhetoric makes words strong. Use it to turn truths strong, not falsities strong. There are four categories of language: weak and wrong, strong and wrong, weak and true, strong and true. Turn weak and true language into strong and true language. Don't turn weak and wrong language into strong and wrong language, weak and true language into strong and wrong language, or strong and true language into weak and true language. Research. Question your assumptions. Strive for truth. Ensure your logic is impeccable. Defuse your biases.

START WITH FINDING TRUTH. The rhetorical endeavor starts with becoming as knowledgeable on your subject as possible and developing an impeccable logical argument. The more research you do, the more rhetoric you earn the right to use.

PUT TRUTH BEFORE STYLE. Rhetorical skill does not make you correct. Truth doesn't care about your rhetoric. If your rhetoric is brilliant, but you realize your arguments are simplistic, flawed, or biased, change course. Let logic lead style. Don't sacrifice logic to style. Don't express bad ideas well. Distinguish effective speaking from effective rational argument. Achieve both, but put reason and logic first.

AVOID THE POPULARITY VORTEX. As Plato suggested, avoid "giving the citizens what they want [in speech] with no thought to whether they will be better or worse as a result of what you are saying." Ignore the temptation to gain positive reinforcement and instant gratification from the audience with no merit to your message. Rhetoric is unethical if used solely to appeal rather than to help the world.

CONSIDER THE CONSEQUENCES. If you succeed to persuade people, will the world become better or worse? Will your audience benefit? Will you benefit? Moreover, is it the best action they could take? Or would an alternative help more? Is it an objectively worthwhile investment? Is it the best solution? Are you giving them all the facts they need to determine this on their own?

CONSIDER SECOND- AND THIRD-ORDER IMPACTS. Consider not only immediate consequences, but consequences across time. Consider the impact of the action you seek to persuade, as well as the tools you use to persuade it. Maybe the action is objectively positive, but in motivating the action, you resorted to instilling beliefs that will cause damage over time. Consider their long-term impact as well.

KNOW THAT BAD ACTORS ARE PLAYING THE SAME GAME. Bad actors already know how to be persuasive and how to spread their lies. They already know the tools. And many lies are more tempting than truth and easier to believe by their very nature. Truth waits for us to find it at the bottom of a muddy well. Truth is complicated, and complexity is harder to convey with impact. Use these tools to give truth a fighting chance in an arena where bad actors have a natural advantage. Use your knowledge to counter and defuse these tools when people misuse them.

APPLY THE FIVE ETHICAL APPROACHES: seek the greatest good for the greatest number (utilitarian); protect the rights of those affected and treat people not as means but as ends (rights); treat equals equally and nonequals fairly (justice); set the good of humanity as the basis of your moral reasoning (common good); act consistently with the ideals that lead to your self-actualization and the highest potential of your character (virtue). Say and do what is right, not what is expedient, and be willing to suffer the consequences of doing so. Don't place self-gratification, acquisitiveness, social status, and power over the common good of all humanity.

APPLY THE FOUR ETHICAL DECISION-MAKING CRITERIA: respect for individual rights to make choices, hold views, and act based on personal beliefs and values (autonomy); the maximization of benefits and the minimization of harms, acting for the benefit of others, helping others further their legitimate interests; taking action to prevent or remove possible harms (beneficence); acting in ways that cause no harm, avoid the risk of harm, and assuring benefits outweigh costs (non-maleficence); treating others according to a defensible standard (justice).

USE ILLOGICAL PROCESSES TO GET ETHICAL RESULTS. Using flawed thinking processes to get good outcomes is not unethical. Someone who disagrees should stop speaking with conviction, clarity, authority, and effective paralanguage. All are irrelevant to the truth of their words, but impact the final judgment of the audience. You must use logic and evidence to figure out the truth. But this doesn't mean logic and evidence will persuade others. Humans have two broad categories of cognitive functions: system one is intuitive, emotional, fast, heuristic-driven, and generally illogical; system two is rational, deliberate, evidence-driven, and generally logical. The best-case scenario is to get people to believe right things for right reasons (through system two). The next best case is to get people to believe right things for wrong reasons (through system one). Both are far better than letting people believe wrong things for wrong reasons. If you don't use those processes, they still function, but lead people astray. You can reverse-engineer them. If you know the truth, have an abundance of reasons to be confident you know the truth, and can predict the disasters that will occur if people don't believe the truth, don't you have a responsibility to be as effective as possible in bringing people to the truth? Logic and evidence are essential, of course. They will persuade many. They should have persuaded you. But people can't always follow a long chain of reasoning or a complicated argument. Persuade by eloquence what you learned by reason.

HELP YOUR SELF-INTEREST. (But not at the expense of your audience or without their knowledge). Ethics calls for improving the world, and you are a part of the world – the one you control most. Improving yourself is a service to others.

APPLY THE WINDOWPANE STANDARD. In Aristotle's view, rhetoric reveals how to persuade and how to defeat manipulative persuaders. Thus, top students of rhetoric would be master speakers, trained to anticipate and disarm the rhetorical tactics of their adversaries. According to this tradition, language is only useful to the extent that it does not distort reality, and good writing functions as a "windowpane," helping people peer through the wall of ignorance and view reality. You might think this precludes persuasion. You might think this calls for dry academic language. But what good is a windowpane if nobody cares to look through it? What good is a windowpane to reality if, on the other wall, a stained-glass window distorts reality but draws people to it? The best windowpane reveals as much of reality as possible while drawing as many people to it as possible.

RUN THROUGH THESE INTROSPECTIVE QUESTIONS. Are the means truly unethical or merely distasteful, unpopular, or unwise? Is the end truly good, or does it simply appear good because we desire it? Is it probable that bad means will achieve the good end? Is the same good achievable using more ethical means if we are creative, patient, and skillful? Is the good end clearly and overwhelmingly better than any bad effects of the means used to attain it? Will the use of unethical means to achieve a good end withstand public scrutiny? Could the use of unethical means be justified to those most affected and those most impartial? Can I specify my ethical criteria or standards? What is the grounding of the ethical judgment? Can I justify the reasonableness and relevancy of these standards for this case? Why are these the best criteria? Why do they take priority? How does the communication succeed or fail by these standards? What judgment is justified in this case about the degree of ethicality? Is it a narrowly focused one rather than a broad and generalized one? To whom is ethical responsibility owed – to which individuals, groups, organizations, or professions? In what ways and to what extent? Which take precedence? What is my responsibility to myself and society? How do I feel about myself after this choice? Can I continue to "live with myself?" Would I want my family to know of this choice? Does the choice reflect my ethical character? To what degree is it "out of character?" If called upon in public to justify the ethics of my communication, how adequately could I do so? What generally accepted reasons could I offer? Are there precedents which can guide me? Are there aspects of this case that set it apart from others? How thoroughly have alternatives been explored before settling on this choice? Is it less ethical than some of the workable alternatives? If the goal requires unethical communication, can I abandon the goal (Johannesen et al., 2007)?

VIEW YOURSELF AS A GUIDE. Stories have a hero, a villain who stands in his way, and a guide who helps the hero fulfill his mission. If you speak ineffectively, you are a nonfactor. If you speak deceitfully, you become the villain. But if you convey truth effectively, you become the guide in your audience's story, who leads them, teaches them, inspires them, and helps them overcome adversity and win. Use your words to put people on the best possible path. And if you hide an ugly truth, ask yourself this: "If I found out that *my* guide omitted this, how would I react?"

APPLY THE PUZZLE ANALOGY. Think of rhetoric as a piece in the puzzle of reality. Only use a rhetorical approach if it fits with the most logical, rational, and evidence-based view of reality. If it doesn't, it's the wrong puzzle piece. Try another.

KNOW THAT THE TRUTH WILL OUT. The truth can either come out in your words, or you can deceive people. You can convince them to live in a fantasy. And that might work. Until. Until truth breaks down the door and storms the building. Until the facade comes crashing down and chaos makes its entry. Slay the dragon in its lair before it comes to your village. Invite truth in through the front door before truth burns the building down. Truth wins in the end, either because a good person spreads, defends, and fights for it, or because untruth reveals itself as such by its consequences, and does so in brutal and painful fashion, hurting innocents and perpetrators alike. Trust and reputation take years to create and seconds to destroy.

MAXIMIZE THE TWO HIERARCHIES OF SUCCESS: honesty *and* effectiveness. You could say "Um, well, uh, I think that um, what we should... should uh... do, is that, well... let me think... er, I think if we are more, you know... fluid, we'll be better at... producing, I mean, progressing, and producing, and just more generally, you know, getting better results, but... I guess my point is, like, that, that if we are more fluid and do things more better, we will get better results than with a bureaucracy and, you know how it is, a silo-based structure, right? I mean... you know what I mean." Or, you could say "Bravery beats bureaucracy, courage beats the status quo, and innovation beats stagnation." Is one of those statements truer? No. Is one of them more effective? Is one of them more likely to get positive action that instantiates the truth into the world? Yes. Language is not reality. It provides signposts to reality. Two different signposts can point at the same truth – they can be equally and maximally true – and yet one can be much more effective. One gets people to follow the road. One doesn't. Maximize honesty. Then, insofar as it doesn't sacrifice honesty, maximize effectiveness. Speak truth. And speak it well.

KNOW THAT DECEPTION SINKS THE SHIP. Deception prevents perception. If someone deceives everyone onboard a ship, blinding them in a sense, they may get away with self-serving behavior. But eventually, they get hurt by the fate they designed. The ship sinks. How could it not? The waters are hazardous. If the crew is operating with distorted perceptions, they fail to see the impending dangers in the deep. So it is with teams, organizations, and entire societies.

APPLY THE WISDOM OF THIS QUOTE. Mary Beard, an American historian, author, and activist, captured the essence of ethical rhetoric well: "What politicians do is they never get the rhetoric wrong, and the price they pay is they don't speak the truth as they see it. Now, I will speak truth as I see it, and sometimes I don't get the rhetoric right. I think that's a fair trade-off." It's more than fair. It's necessary.

REMEMBER YOUR RESPONSIBILITY TO SOCIETY. Be a guardian of the truth. Speak out against wrongdoing, and do it well. The solution to evil speech is not less speech, but more (good) speech. Create order with your words, not chaos. Our civilization depends on it. Match the truth, honesty, and vulnerable transparency of your words against the irreducible complexity of the universe. And in this complex universe, remember the omnipresence of nuance, and the dangers of simplistic ideologies. (Inconveniently, simplistic ideologies are persuasive, while nuanced truths are difficult to convey. This is why good people need to be verbally skilled; to pull the extra weight of conveying a realistic worldview). Don't commit your whole mind to an isolated fragment of truth, lacking context, lacking nuance. Be precise in your speech, to ensure you are saying what you mean to say. Memorize the logical fallacies, the cognitive biases, and the rules of logic and correct thinking. (Conveniently, many rhetorical devices are also reasoning devices that focus your inquiry and help you explicate truth). But don't demonize those with good intentions and bad ideas. If they are forthcoming and honest, they are not your enemy. Rather, the two of you are on a shared mission to find the truth, partaking in a shared commitment to reason and dialogue. The malevolent enemy doesn't care about the truth. And in this complex world, remember Voltaire's warning to "cherish those who seek the truth but beware of those who find it," and Aristotle's startling observation that "the least deviation from truth [at the start] is multiplied a thousandfold." Be cautious in determining what to say with conviction. Good speaking is not a substitute for good thinking. The danger zone is being confidently incorrect. What hurts us most is what we know that just isn't so. Remember these tenets and your responsibility, and rhetoric becomes the irreplaceable aid of the good person doing good things in difficult times; the sword of the warrior of the light.

KNOW THAT DECEPTION IS ITS OWN PUNISHMENT. Knowingly uttering a falsehood is a spoken lie of commission. Having something to say but not saying it is a spoken lie of omission. Knowingly behaving inauthentically is an acted-out lie of commission. Knowingly omitting authentic behavior is an acted-out lie of omission. All these deceptions weaken your being. All these deceptions corrupt your own mind, turning your greatest asset into an ever-present companion you can no longer trust. Your conscience operates somewhat autonomously, and it will call you out (unless your repeated neglect desensitizes it). You have a conscious conscience which speaks clearly, and an unconscious conscience, which communicates more subtly. A friend of mine asked: "Why do we feel relieved when we speak truth? Why are we drawn toward it, even if it is not pleasant? Do our brains have something that makes this happen?" Yes, they do: our consciences, our inner lights, our inner north stars. And we feel relieved because living with the knowledge of our own deceit is often an unbearable burden. You live your life before an audience of one: yourself. You cannot escape the observation of your own awareness; you can't hide from yourself. Everywhere you go, there you are. Everything you do, there you are. Some of the greatest heights of wellbeing come from performing well in this one-man theater, and signaling virtue to yourself; being someone you are proud to be (and grateful to observe). Every time you lie, you tell your subconscious mind that your character is too weak to contend with the truth. And this shapes your character accordingly. It becomes true. And then what? Lying carries its own punishment, even if the only person who catches the liar is the liar himself.

BE A MONSTER (THEN LEARN TO CONTROL IT). There is nothing moral about weakness and harmlessness. The world is difficult. There are threats to confront, oppressors to resist, and tyrants to rebuff. (Peterson, 2018). There are psychopaths, sociopaths, and Machiavellian actors with no love for the common good. There is genuine malevolence. If you are incapable of being an effective deceiver, then you are incapable of being an effective advocate for truth: it is the same weapon, pointed in different directions. If you cannot use it in both directions, can you use it at all? Become a monster, become dangerous, and become capable of convincing people to believe in a lie... and then use this ability to convince them to believe in the truth. The capacity for harm is also the capacity for harming harmful entities; that is to say, defending innocent ones. If you can't hurt anyone, you can't help anyone when they need someone to stand up for them. Words are truly weapons, and the most powerful weapons in the world at that. The ability to use them, for good *or* for bad, is the prerequisite to using them for good. There is an archetype in our cultural narratives: the well-intentioned but harmless protagonist who gets roundly defeated by the villain, until he develops his monstrous edge and integrates it, at which point he becomes the triumphant hero. Along similar lines, I watched a film about an existential threat to humanity, in which the protagonist sought to convey the threat to a skeptical public, but failed miserably because he lacked the rhetorical skill to do so. The result? The world ended. Everyone died. The protagonist was of no use to anyone. And this almost became a true story. A historical study showed that in the Cuban Missile Crisis, the arguments that won out in the United States mastermind group were not the best, but those argued with the most conviction. Those with the best arguments lacked the skill to match. The world (could have) ended. The moral? Speak truth... well.

MASTERING COMMUNICATION, ONE SKILL AT A TIME

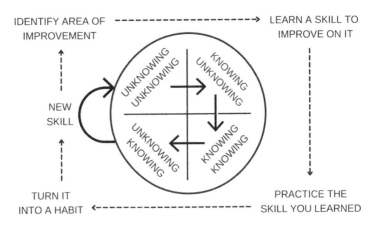

FIGURE I: The proven path to mastery.

influence

....

noun

    the capacity to have an effect on the character,
development, or behavior of someone or something

CONTENTS

THE STRATEGIES: 145

BEFORE YOU GO…

Rhetoric, Motivated by Love, Guided by Reason, and Aimed at Truth, Is a Powerful Force for the Greatest Good.

POLITICAL DISCLAIMER

Throughout this book, and throughout all my books, I draw examples of communication strategies from the political world. I quote from the speeches of many of America's great leaders, like JFK and MLK, as well as from more recent political figures of both major parties. Political communication is ideal for illustrating the concepts revealed in the books. It is the best source of examples of words that work that I have ever found. I don't use anything out of the political mainstream. And it is by extensively studying the inaugural addresses of United States Presidents and the great speeches of history that I have discovered many of the speaking strategies I share with you.

My using the words of any particular figure to illustrate a principle of communication is not necessarily an endorsement of the figure or their message. Separate the speaker from the strategy. After all, the strategy is the only reason the speaker made an appearance in the book at all. Would you rather have a weak example of a strategy you want to learn from a speaker you love, or a perfect example of the strategy from a speaker you detest?

For a time, I didn't think a disclaimer like this was necessary. I thought people would do this on their own. I thought that if people read an example of a strategy drawn from the words of a political figure they disagreed with, they would appreciate the value of the example as an instructive tool and set aside their negative feelings about the speaker. "Yes, I don't agree with this speaker or the message, but I can clearly see the strategy in this example and I now have a better understanding of how it works and how to execute it." Indeed, I suspect 95% of my readers do just that. You probably will, too. But if you are part of the 5% who aren't up for it, don't say I didn't warn you, and please don't leave a negative review because you think I endorse this person or that person. I don't, as this is strictly a book about communication.

INFLUENCE

THE PSYCHOLOGY OF WORDS THAT
WIN HEARTS AND CHANGE MINDS

SPEAK FOR SUCCESS COLLECTION BOOK

INFLUENCE CHAPTER

I

GUARANTEED INFLUENCE:

Why We Know these Tactics Win Hearts and Change Minds

WHAT DO YOU HOLD IN YOUR HANDS?

W HY DOES IT MATTER? WHY DO YOU need to communicate? How will it help you?

A better question is "how won't it help you?"

You need to communicate to succeed. Weak communication skills will condemn your ideas to a slow and painful death in your mind. An idea born in your mind wants, above all else, to grow; to spread from mind to mind, until a critical mass of persuaded people makes it happen in reality. How can your brilliant idea move from mind to mind if not by communication? And what better way to guarantee it spreads than effective communication?

Effective communication – in other words, communication that uses the strategies I will teach you in this book – is what sets otherwise similar people apart: middle-managers and CEOs, mediocre salesmen and top performers, the 119 people who interviewed, and the one who got the job.

Those who speak well do well. Those who influence with grace lead with strength. Those who persuade with subtle strategy sell with stunning ease. Those who communicate like experts are respected like experts.

And let me ask you this: What would you rather be seen as? What do you want the people making decisions about your pay, your future, and your work to think of you? That you are capable of leading, or not? That you can change the minds of others, or not? That you are an expert, or not? That you are competent at the one skill that counts, or not? That you can communicate exceptionally and thus succeed exceptionally, or not?

The key to the minds of those you need to influence to get what you want is often the right word, and if not the right word, the right set of words, combined in the right way, spoken in the right way, and delivered at the right time.

It's so simple and easy. It's within your reach. If you're reading these words right now, and go on to read this book cover to cover, the power of communication will be yours. The secret of success – or rather, one of the particularly important secrets of success – will be unlocked.

And what, specifically, is this secret to success? Let us assume that success is turning reality from what it is to what you want it to be. How would you do that, if not by selecting a favorite idea, and communicating it effectively to one, then ten, then one-hundred people? How would you do that if not by replicating in the minds of others the immense belief in the idea that exists in yours?

COMMUNICATION EMPOWERS YOUR SUCCESS

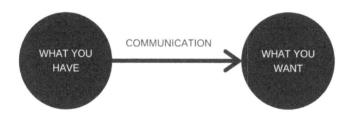

FIGURE 1: Communication is a critical component of success; of turning what you have into what you want.

The people who get ahead, and live the lives they want to live, are the people who can take an idea they love, and manifest it in the real world. And the people who can do that are the people who can communicate. And the people who can communicate are the people who use the secrets in this book. Stick with me. You'll be glad you did. Don't give up the pursuit of success. The moment you give up the pursuit of perfect communication, you inherently give up the pursuit of success as well. Success demands communication. Succeeding in manifesting an idea demands that others are aware of the idea, impassioned by it, and excited to help you bring it into being.

So, how did I create this book you hold in your hands? How did I discover the secrets of communication that you'll find buried in it? How did I find out the proven secrets of communication that changes minds and influences people?

The mission of my life, at least this part of my life, is to arm the world's good and ambitious people with the communication tools they need to turn their good ambitions into their beautiful realities. There are three principal ways I do that.

SECRETS OF HUMAN PSYCHOLOGY

The human mind works in certain ways, and effective communication plays upon these mechanisms of human psychology. Many of the secrets you will learn in this book are the result of taking the latest groundbreaking psychological study, and applying its lessons to communication. If you want to communicate to humans, you must communicate in a way that plays upon the inherent intricacies of the human mind. I will teach you exactly how to do this in a way nobody else will. Instead of giving you useless and shallow best practices based on some weak intuition, I give you proven and bullet-proof techniques built upon an infallible foundation: the mechanisms of psychology.

KEY INSIGHT:

Rhetorical Strategies Work Because of Human Psychology.

UNPACKING THE MECHANISMS OF HUMAN PSYCHOLOGY

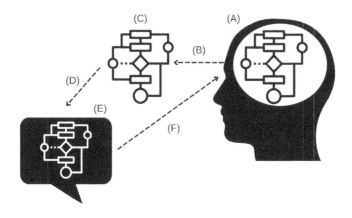

FIGURE 2: The human mind is filled with predictable, algorithmic through processes (A). I learn (B) and simplify these thought processes (C), applying them to communication (D) and developing communication models (E) that appeal to them (F).

METHODS OF PERSONAL EXPERIENCE

I have given hundreds of presentations on hundreds of subjects to thousands of people. I have narrowed down communication fact from fiction; I have broken down effective communication to its guaranteed truths, and ignored the rest. I have ignored what worked once, twice, ten, or even fifty times for me, and only accepted what worked every single time, under every single circumstance, speaking about every single subject, to every single audience. In addition, I' have broken down not only what worked for me, but what worked for my hundreds of students too. I have controlled for every single lurking variable: speaker, audience, subject, and circumstance being the most notable. And from this methodology, I draw not wishy-washy pieces of circumstantial advice, but proven strategies that work.

ANALYZING MY PERSONAL EXPERIENCE

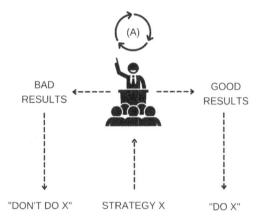

FIGURE 3: I try strategy X. I try it multiple times (A). If I get good results, I incorporate the strategy. If I get bad results, I tell you to avoid the strategy or mistake.

THE STRATEGY OF REVERSE-ENGINEERING

I'm pretty great at this stuff. But I have a coach that knows everything about communication that there is to know. I have a coach who makes my experience look like dirt; like nothing; like useless garbage. I have a coach who makes the experience of the top 100 communication coaches in the United States combined look like dirt; like nothing; like useless garbage. I have a coach who has the aggregate experience of every single major piece of communication ever created at the ready.

Who is this coach? I just said it: every single major piece of communication ever created. So, why don't you go to this coach instead? Because it is incredibly difficult and arduous to work with him; he demands dedication and effort, and only after spending a significant amount of time with him will he give you a small golden nugget of communication wisdom. It would be far more efficient for one person to work with this coach and then pass on his wisdom to a general audience, than for everyone to get it on their own. I'm that person.

THE WORLD'S MOST IMPACTFUL SPEAKING COACH

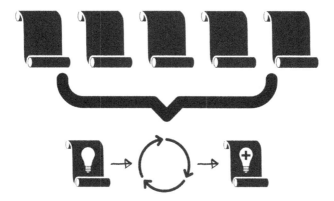

FIGURE 4: I analyze the legendary messages of legendary leaders and extrapolate communication algorithms from them: proven, step-by-step processes that turn a "starting message" into a superior version of itself.

MASTERY VISUALIZED

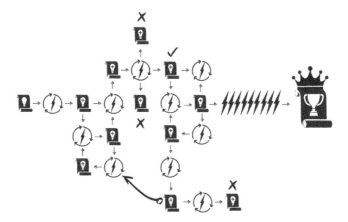

FIGURE 5: Communication mastery is the result of chaining these algorithms together.

So, if you're ever wondering how I discovered one of these communication strategies, and it's not psychology or personal experience, it is by reverse-engineering the legendary speeches of history to discover their secrets. I didn't do this at the beginning of my career as a public speaking coach, but I wish I had.

Let me show you how this strategy revealed to me the foundation of all effective communication: the public speaking triad (the connections between the speaker, the audience, and the subject).

KEY INSIGHT:

The Most Important Part of Successful Communication Is the Speaker-Audience Connection.

This Connection Is the Foundation For Consensus, Influence, And Progress.

In a debate between George W. Bush and Bill Clinton, when asked a question regarding how the national debt had affected them in their lives, Bush stuttered in response and answered quite coldly and without emotion, within the one-yard radius around his stool and podium. Clinton, on the other hand, left his podium and advanced toward the audience. He made eye contact, intensely narrowed his eyes, and described with highly inclusive language how the national debt has affected all Americans including himself.

You're going to see the incredible difference. It's huge. What happened at that town hall debate connects so many aspects of this book, from the basic public speaking triad to eye contact, facial expression, and so much more you will learn in the use of voice, use of body, and aspects of delivery sections. Let's take a much deeper analysis of the speeches. This is exactly what happened at the famous debate moment between Bush and the audience, stutters included:

Audience member: "How has the national debt personally affected each of your lives and if it hasn't how can you honestly find a cure for the economic problems of the common people if you have no experience in what's ailing them?" [Audience member is seeking information and a connection to the speaker. She was already connected to the idea; she may not have thought of it this way, but what the candidates were prompted to do by her question was to connect themselves to her and to the idea].

Bush: "Well I think the national debt affects everybody, uh, obviously it has a lot to do with interest rates, it has –" [Bush starts off on the wrong foot by not directly addressing the question, which the moderator points out. He is lacking a connection to both the idea and the audience member at this point].

Moderator: "She's saying you personally." [Need of the moderator to clarify emphasizes the broken public speaking triad: the speaker and the audience member are disconnected].

Audience member: "Yes, on a personal basis, how has it affected you?" [Audience member tries to form the connection to the speaker again and prompts the speaker to connect himself to the idea which she feels connected to].

Bush: "Well, I'm sure it has, I love my grandchildren, I want to think that –" [Bush struggles to form the connection to the idea, and chooses a very non-compelling example. He doesn't use any inclusive language either].

Audience member: "How?" [Audience member, once again, tries to make the connection].

Bush: "I want to think that they're going to be able to afford an education, I think that that's an important part of being a parent – I, if the question, if you're sa – maybe I won't get it wrong, are you suggesting that if somebody has means, that the national debt doesn't affect them?"

[Bush continues struggling trying to connect himself to the idea and audience member; the public speaking triad remains broken, and he employs little to no inclusive language to try to reconnect it].

Audience member: "Well what I'm saying is –" [Audience member tries rephrasing, and Bush interrupts].

Bush: "I – I'm not sure I get it, help me with the question and I'll try to answer." [Bush, instead of finding a way to connect himself to the audience member and to the idea, asks her to rephrase the question even though she already made it clear several times].

Audience member: "Well I have friends that have been laid off from jobs." [She tries to prod for a connection here].

Bush: "Yeah" [Bush attempts a filler word, which doesn't sound good at this particular moment].

Audience member: "I know people who cannot afford to pay the mortgage on their homes, their car payment, I have personal –" [She continues trying to prod for a connection both between herself and Bush, and Bush and the idea of the national debt and its impact on each candidate].

Bush: "Yeah" [Another filler word].

Audience member: "– problems with the national debt, but how has it affected you? And if you have no experience in it, how can you help us? If you don't know what we're feeling?" [Bush still did not find a way to connect himself to the speaker and to the idea].

Moderator: "I think she means more the recession, the economic problems today the country faces rather than the national debt" [Moderator facilitating the connection between speaker, idea, and audience member emphasizes the broken public speaking triad yet again].

Up until this point, what is most evident is simply a broken public speaking triad. The lack of inclusive, relatable, and positive language becomes more evident once Bush picks a direction:

BUSH SUFFERED FROM A BROKEN PUBLIC SPEAKING TRIAD

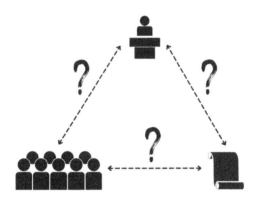

FIGURE 6: Bush failed to form the three-way connection between speaker, audience, and subject / message.

Bush: "Well listen, you oughta, you oughta be in the white house for a day [Bush attempts a very non-inclusive and non-relatable response: how can the audience member relate to what's going on in the white house?] and hear what I hear and see what I see and read the mail I read, and touch the people that I touch from time to time. [Bush finally begins to describe his personal experiences with the national debt, but once again struggles to make a deliberate connection between himself and the idea, and abruptly shifts approaches] – I was in the low max, AME church, it's a black church, just outside of Washington D.C., and I read in the bulletin, about teenage pregnancies, about the difficulty that families are having to meet ends – make ends meet, I've talked to parents [The audience member is likely thinking "Okay, but what does that have to do with you? You've interacted with people affected by the national debt, but how does that deliberately connect you to it?" This is barely inclusive]. I mean, you've gotta care. Everybody cares if people aren't doing well [Again, the question doesn't have to do with how everybody has been affected, but how Bush has been affected]. But I don't think, I don't think it's fair to say you haven't had cancer therefore you don't know what it's like [Non-inclusive language that alienates the audience member even further from Bush by saying her question was unfair]. I don't think it's fair, uhh, you know whatever it is that you haven't been hit by personally, but everybody's affected by the debt ['Everybody' is a poor substitute for the much more inclusive and personal pronoun "we." Bush was unable to do the most important thing at this point: framing the issue as something directly inclusive (a 'we problem') instead of as something remotely inclusive (an 'everybody problem')]. because of the tremendous interest that goes into paying on that debt, everything's more expensive, everything comes out of your pocket and my pocket [Instead of emphasizing the separation between 'your pocket' and 'my pocket,' why not say 'our pockets'?], so it's, it's set, but I think in terms of the recession, of course you feel it when you're the president of the United States [Very non-inclusive: how can the audience member possibly relate to being the president?], that's why I'm trying to do something about it by stimulating the export, investing more, better education system. Thank you, I'm glad to clarify."

Bush's response suffered from a broken public speaking triad (he did not connect speaker, audience, and subject) and an absence of relatable, inclusive language. Not only that, but the initial confusion and lack of connection between him, the idea, and the audience member threw him off. When he finally got on track, he was not quite as eloquent as he may have otherwise been. Clinton does not repeat Bush's mistakes.

Clinton: "Tell me how it's affected you again?" [He starts off on the right foot. Clinton, at this point, was trying to re-identify the connection between audience member and idea, so that he could present to her a similar connection between himself and the idea].

Audience member: "Uhm..." [Audience member is evidently caught off guard by the sudden connection to the speaker, after a few minutes when it was absent with the previous speaker].

Clinton: "You know people who've lost their jobs –" [Clinton notices her off-guardedness, and lends a helping hand, bolstering the speaker to audience connection yet further].

Audience member: "Well yeah" [Clinton gets the audience member agreeing with him, even on a matter of clarification, right off the bat].

Clinton: "And lost their homes?" [He continues by saying what the audience member was likely thinking. This goes a very long way to developing the speaker to audience connection].

Audience member: "Mhm" [The speaker to audience connection is complete at this point. Clinton made it clear that unlike Bush, he understands her situation very well. He proceeds, with this clear understanding of her situation, to relate himself to it in an inclusive and relatable way].

Clinton: "Well, I've been governor of a small state for 12 years. [Clinton keeps the background information concise, but also subtly draws attention to his experience]. I'll tell you how it's affected me personally. [He immediately commits himself to answering her question clearly and unambiguously]. Every year, congress - and the president sign laws that makes us [us, not me] – make us do more things and gives us [us, not me] less money to do it with. I see people in my state, middle class people; their taxes have gone up in

Washington and their services have gone down, while the wealthy have gotten tax cuts. [This may be misleading: it is indeed a lot of "I." However, it is Clinton describing to the audience member how her situation has been occurring to people in his state for a very long time]. I have seen what's happened in this last four years, when – in my state, when people lose their jobs there's a good chance I'll know em' by their names. When a factory closes, I know the people who ran it. When the businesses go bankrupt, I know them. [This is perhaps the best example of Clinton's mastery of inclusive language. He is saying in a very compelling way, that "I know people just like you in my state. I have spent the past 12 years working to help them. I have, every day, seen people affected by this, and because I am their governor, I was affected by it myself."] And I've been out here for thirteen months, meeting in meetings just like this ever since October, with people like you all over America; people that have lost their jobs, lost their livelihoods, lost their health insurance. [Highly inclusive once again: he makes a clear effort to describe some of the struggles people are facing. Some of the very struggles she identified in her question]. What I want you to understand is, the national debt is not the only cause of that. [He pivots after connecting himself to the speaker and to the idea. This speech is technically one to inform and persuade, and now that he completed the public speaking triad, he begins working to accomplish those goals]. It is because America has not invested in its people; it is because we [directly inclusive language] have not grown; it is because we've had twelve years of trickle-down economics. We've gone from first to twelfth in the world in wages, we've had four years when we produced no private sector jobs, most people are working harder for less money than they were making ten years ago. It is because we are in the grip of a failed economic theory. And this decision you're about to make better be about what kind of economic theory you want; not just people sayin' I wanna go fix it, but what are we going to do! What I think we have to do is invest in American jobs, American education, control American healthcare costs, and bring the American people together again. [more directly inclusive language, also ending on a very positive note]."

Let's compare Bush and Clinton's approaches. From the start, the audience member was connected to the idea: struggling economically due to the national debt. The sentiment of her question, then, was essentially: "Which candidate can better connect to me and my struggles due to the national debt?"

Bush did not connect to her and her struggles. Clinton methodically connected himself to the audience member, and then proceeded to connect himself to the idea. In doing so, he completed the public speaking triad. Inclusive and relatable language is one of the biggest tools he used to establish these connections.

In the larger segment of Bush's speech, when he finally got his footing, he used only two vaguely inclusive and relatable statements: "I was in the low max, AME church, it's a black church, just outside of Washington D.C., and I read in the bulletin, about teenage pregnancies, about the difficulty that families are having to meet ends – make ends meet, I've talked to parents..." and "everything comes out of your pocket and my pocket." Clinton, on the other hand, used 13 highly inclusive and relatable statements. Additionally, Clinton ended on a very positive note: bringing the American people together again. Bush didn't end on a negative note, but not on a particularly positive one either.

Above and beyond inclusive language, Clinton was suave, spoke eloquently, had intense stage presence, and made use of at least 57 of the public speaking principles shared in this book.

Who do you think got that lady's vote? Who do you think got the votes of a large group of Americans who felt the same way as her, and had the same question? It was probably the same candidate who won that election by six million votes. Bill Clinton.

When I go to this coach seeking communication wisdom, what he really does is select another coach for me. In this case, I got two coaches: Clinton and Bush. And they taught me (and my readers and students) an incredible amount about communication. They gave me a side-by-side comparison of effective communication and ineffective (or rather comparatively less effective) communication. It was beautiful. And having read that, you see how much communication wisdom we can extract from these examples.

Sometimes I hit a goldmine. For example, I have an analysis of a speech by JFK that gave me about one hundred communication strategies. And these strategies were excellent; they were specific formulas that organize your words in the most powerful, eloquent, and compelling way possible.

But it gets better: I never rely on one method of discovering these secrets. I cross-reference human psychology, my experience, and the wisdom gained through reverse engineering all with each other. This is why I am so confident, and why I call these strategies "guaranteed." Why? Because I treat this like a science, not just as an art. And what is an art, if not proven processes used with practiced skill, plus the correct energy and mindset?

KEY INSIGHT:

The Best Art Conceals Itself. The Overwhelming Majesty of the Sistine Chapel Hides Its Brushstrokes Behind Perfection.

MY THREE-PRONGED APPROACH TO COMMUNICATION

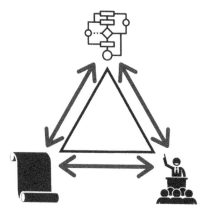

FIGURE 7: I combine my personal experience, the reverse-engineering of psychology, and the reverse-engineering of legendary messages to discover and compile patterns of communication that work. The evidentiary basis for my advice is – and I say this humbly – drastically stronger than that of most authors on this subject, who typically rely on one of these three ingredients.

I may not be the best expert on this subject. But I'll tell you this: I am the best at applying a near-scientific process at drawing wisdom about this subject from psychology, experience, and examples. You'll become a master at the art of communication when the scientific processes of effective communication are buried so deep into your subconscious mind that they happen effortlessly. And the first step is learning them.

What separates the master communicator – the JFKs and MLKs of the world – from someone who understands the same technical communication strategies, perhaps by reading about them? It is whether or not those processes are deeply burrowed in the subconscious mind. Why? Because once they are, they become a part of you, and it is this unification that creates such effortlessly incredible communication.

THE TWO STEPS TO COMMUNICATION MASTERY

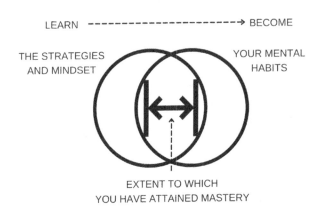

FIGURE 8: First, learn the strategies. Then, become them. You attain mastery when the strategies and the mindset supporting them are mirrored by your mental habits.

The worst case is to not use any of the secrets in this book. A vastly better case is to use them all purposefully. The best case is to use them without meaning to; naturally, effortlessly, and masterfully, because they are deeply burrowed in your subconscious mind, and are a matter of thoughtless habit.

Every single thing I could have done to better facilitate this subconscious transmutation for you, I did. Why? Because that is what will truly make you the best communicator that you can become; a communicator who effortlessly, through habitual and thoughtless action, persuades people, morphs minds, and achieves influence.

These actions on my part include using certain composition elements to help you retain, in long-term memory, the techniques. For example, I implemented the strategy of "chunking" the book into many smaller, shorter segments, which particularly empowers subconscious retention. They also include simplifying the information in every way possible to ensure that there are no unnecessary details distracting from the necessary ones – in other words, presenting the information in the most subconsciously intuitive way. But they include, most importantly, repeating at different times and in different words the most critical concepts that must absolutely become incontrovertibly natural to you. Repeated thought impulses are significantly more likely to be remembered, taken up by your conscious mind, and then subconsciously adopted than one-and-done thought impulses. Your actions are produced by your thoughts; the right thoughts produce the right actions that produce the right reactions (results from the world). Wrong thoughts yield wrong actions and wrong reactions. How do you create the right "automatic" or habitual thoughts and the right actions that they in turn create (thus yielding the desired results)? Here's how: with deliberate repetition of the inalienably powerful truths relevant to the matter at hand. Almost every self-improvement author I've read indisputably, unequivocally, and beyond all doubt, agrees on this.

WHAT IS THE HABIT LOOP?

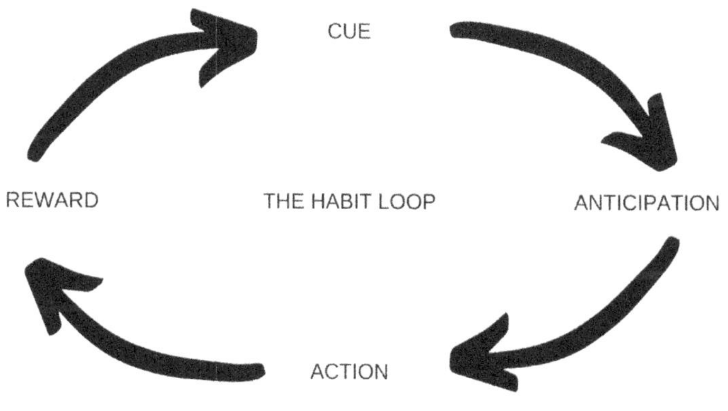

FIGURE 9: This is the habit loop. A cue leads to anticipation of reward that results in action and reward.

HOW THE HABIT LOOP CREATES MASTERY

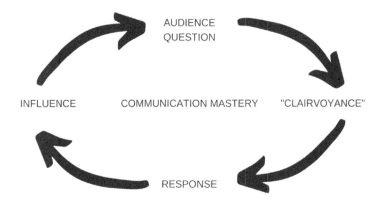

FIGURE 10: These communication strategies must enter your being in the form of habit loops. This is what is meant by "become the strategies." For example, if you get an audience question, you will instantly anticipate the best response ("clairvoyance"), provide the response, and attain the reward of immense influence, eloquence, impact, inspiration, etc. The world's legendary communicators speak effortlessly because of their habit loops.

UNPACKING THE FLOW STATE

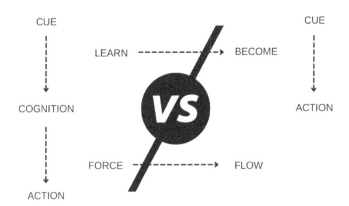

FIGURE 11: What is called a "flow state" is really just a near-instant link between cue and action.

In short, rest assured: The things that must be drilled into your head for successful communication will be drilled into your head, by me, through repetition.

HOW THIS BOOK IS ORGANIZED

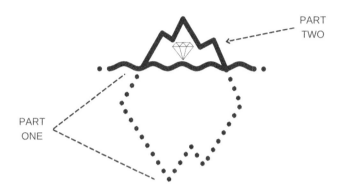

FIGURE 12: In the first half of the book we discuss Monroe's Motivated Sequence – the foundational five-step structure of influence. In the second half of the book we discuss advanced strategies to layer on top of Monroe's Motivated Sequence. The first half of the book includes diagrams that visualize the steps of the sequence in such a way that your retention and intuitive understanding of the process significantly improve. The first half of the book is designed – based on the proven principles of information retention – to empower your memory of the five steps.

After you read this book, you will never forget the things that you cannot afford to forget. This book is deliberately designed to form your habit loops, taking you drastically closer to mastery. Part of that is repetition, part of that is presentation, part of that is organization, but it all serves the same goal: helping you attain communication mastery.

........................Chapter Summary........................

- Speaking in a compelling, captivating, and persuasive manner is one of the most crucial skills for succeeding.
- I derive the content of my books in three ways: personal experience, psychology, and reverse-engineering.
- I rely on elements of my personal experience, but this alone is rarely a fully sufficient "sample size."
- I study psychology and apply the findings to speech and communication. These strategies are scientific.
- I reverse-engineer the legendary words of legendary leaders, abstracting adaptable strategies from the specifics.
- Most of the strategies, dictums, and advice revealed in this book includes an example, usually from a U.S. President.

KEY INSIGHT:

The Foundational Persuasive Structure Sets the Stage for Sophisticated Strategies.

Stack the Strategies In Part Two Atop the Five Steps of the Structure Revealed In Part One.

THREE POWERFUL MODES OF INFLUENCE

ASPIRATIONAL INFLUENCE

We could be here.

We are here.

CONTRAST INFLUENCE

This is way better...

...than this.

CROSSROADS INFLUENCE

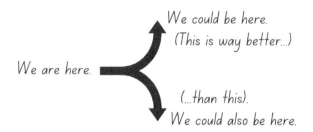

We could be here.
(This is way better...)

We are here.

(...than this).
We could also be here.

THREE POWERFUL OPENINGS

IF-THEN

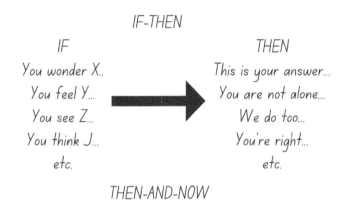

IF	THEN
You wonder X..	This is your answer...
You feel Y...	You are not alone...
You see Z...	We do too...
You think J...	You're right...
etc.	etc.

THEN-AND-NOW

X LONG AGO

Things were like this.

NOW

They are like this.

A MOMENT OF DECISION

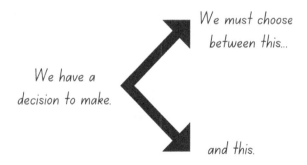

We must choose between this...

We have a decision to make.

and this.

Claim These Free Resources that Will Help You Unleash the Power of Your Words and Speak with Confidence. Visit www.speakforsuccesshub.com/toolkit for Access.

18 Free PDF Resources

12 Iron Rules for Captivating Story, 21 Speeches that Changed the World, 341-Point Influence Checklist, 143 Persuasive Cognitive Biases, 17 Ways to Think On Your Feet, 18 Lies About Speaking Well, 137 Deadly Logical Fallacies, 12 Iron Rules For Captivating Slides, 371 Words that Persuade, 63 Truths of Speaking Well, 27 Laws of Empathy, 21 Secrets of Legendary Speeches, 19 Scripts that Persuade, 12 Iron Rules For Captivating Speech, 33 Laws of Charisma, 11 Influence Formulas, 219-Point Speech-Writing Checklist, 21 Eloquence Formulas

Claim These Free Resources that Will Help You Unleash the Power of Your Words and Speak with Confidence. Visit www.speakforsuccesshub.com/toolkit for Access.

30 Free Video Lessons

We'll send you one free video lesson every day for 30 days, written and recorded by Peter D. Andrei. Days 1-10 cover authenticity, the prerequisite to confidence and persuasive power. Days 11-20 cover building self-belief and defeating communication anxiety. Days 21-30 cover how to speak with impact and influence, ensuring your words change minds instead of falling flat. Authenticity, self-belief, and impact – this course helps you master three components of confidence, turning even the most high-stakes presentations from obstacles into opportunities.

Claim These Free Resources that Will Help You Unleash the Power of Your Words and Speak with Confidence. Visit <u>www.speakforsuccesshub.com/toolkit</u> for Access.

2 Free Workbooks

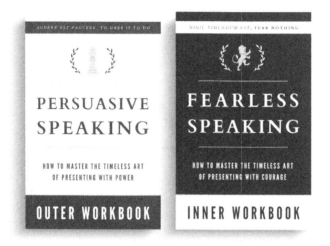

We'll send you two free workbooks, including long-lost excerpts by Dale Carnegie, the mega-bestselling author of *How to Win Friends and Influence People* (5,000,000 copies sold). *Fearless Speaking* guides you in the proven principles of mastering your inner game as a speaker. *Persuasive Speaking* guides you in the time-tested tactics of mastering your outer game by maximizing the power of your words. All of these resources complement the Speak for Success collection.

SPEAK FOR SUCCESS COLLECTION BOOK

INFLUENCE CHAPTER

THE STRUCTURE:
The Foundational Five-Step
Framework of Influence

FIVE STEPS TO INFLUENCE

C OUNTLESS PERSUASIVE MESSAGES FAIL BECAUSE of weak structure. Monroe's Motivated Sequence is an easy, proven persuasive structure that you can use in conversations, presentations, meetings, or interviews. If you want to motivate people to take enthusiastic action, apply this structure.

WHAT IS MONROE'S MOTIVATED SEQUENCE?

Monroe's Motivated Sequence is named after the man who first described it: Alan H. Monroe. He developed it in the 1930s, and ever since then, it has been proven to achieve results.

Why is Monroe's Motivated Sequence so powerful? It places emphasis on a glaring problem the audience faces. It focuses on what the audience can do to solve it. It is a seamless journey through the steps of persuasion. It acts as a gentle "yes ladder" to action. It builds positive persuasive momentum (a series of affirmative "yes" responses to propositions of escalating intensity, starting with the easiest to accept). It is a simple step-by-step process you can apply to any speech. It takes all the confusion out of organization and sequencing. It works for any subject. It is applicable to all persuasive endeavors. It is simple, yet powerful.

WHAT ARE THE FIVE STEPS TO MONROE'S MOTIVATED SEQUENCE?

Grab attention. Present an audience need. Express how you can satisfy the need with a solution. Help them visualize this satisfaction. Propose the requisite action.

ATTENTION

In the attention step, your goal is to get your audience listening to you. This is the job of the hook. You can use a personal anecdote, a dramatic quote, or a statistic. You can use anything that gets your audience's attention. You will shortly learn four proven attention-grabbing methods.

NEED

In the need step, your goal is to establish a clear problem. It must be a clear problem that is directly relevant to your audience. It shouldn't be an abstract, distant problem that affects other people (unless this is the inherent nature of your subject matter – but even then, you should connect it to your audience to the best of your ability). Make it clear to your audience that the problem directly relates to them and their needs. This step-by-step process is instructive: Clearly state the problem. Describe the problem. Describe the impacts of the problem. Clearly connect this problem to your audience in specific terms. You can also use proven desire-instigating techniques.

SATISFACTION

In step two, you created a need. You created a desire. Now, you answer this question: "How do I fulfill my need? How do I satisfy the desire?" In the satisfaction step, your goal is to show your audience a clear solution to the problem outlined in the need step. This is the solution you want them to adopt. It's what you are trying to persuade them to do. Only now is it time to express to your audience what you want them to do. Clearly describe what you are trying to get your audience to adopt. Then connect that to the need by showing how it solves the problem. Prove that the solution solves the problem with evidence, past experiences, and logos (which we will cover). And use the four tension-resolving techniques we will discuss shortly.

VISUALIZATION

In the visualization step, your goal is to help your audience visualize what will happen if they adopt your solution, or what will happen if they don't. You can also show them what will happen if they don't, followed by what will happen if they do, or vice-versa. This is called the contrast method.

And for our last step, the step that is now much more persuasive and powerful because of the four steps preceding it, we turn to the grand finale: action. Without the four preceding steps, it would never work. But the sequence of these steps makes them each significantly more persuasive, compelling, and engaging, culminating in a much higher success-rate when you finally request a specific action.

ACTION

In the action step, your goal is to motivate your audience toward a specific action. What is the first thing they need to do after listening? This is your call to action. But you must circumvent a common obstacle: Even if your audience was with you the entire time, listening, nodding, and smiling, there's still a good chance they won't take the action. Why? Because of human inertia, habit, and cognitive dissonance. But a set of four proven methods will increase the chances of inspiring your audience to follow through.

Attention: Get your audience's attention. Need: Establish a clear, compelling need. Satisfaction: Present a satisfaction of that need. Visualization: Help them visualize the positive outcome. Action: Ask for specific action.

VISUALIZING THE FIVE STEPS OF INFLUENCE

FIGURE 13: Grab attention, present a need, offer satisfaction, inspire visualization, and get action. These are the five steps of the foundational structure of influence.

THE ATTENTION STEP: FOUR SIMPLE METHODS TO EASILY CAPTURE AUDIENCE ATTENTION

No matter the value of your message, the persuasiveness of your content, or the strength of your evidence, it all goes to waste if you can't grab attention when you need it. These four methods show you how. Just like the methods for accomplishing the other steps, you can use one of them once, one of them multiple times, all of them once in whatever sequence you deem fitting, or all of them multiple times. These are the bricks; the tower is yours to build, using the bricks how you see fit insofar as you don't deviate too much from the initial five-step sequence. Of course, the attention step is just the foundation of the tower, upon which the remainder will be built.

USE A STATISTIC

Statistics give you authority and grab attention. However, they have to be understandable, relevant, and shocking statistics.

The third quality is most important: If you want attention, start with a shocking statistic. And avoid the common mistake of starting with a statistic but not giving a "qualitative" example. Numbers are great, but they aren't as intuitive. They aren't as emotional. They aren't as human. Start with a statistic, but then zoom in to one specific example of that statistic (that is emotionally compelling and deeply human).

And don't make the mistake of forgetting to clearly connect the statistic to your claim with "logical warrants." The statistic is your evidence, not your claim. You must show with clear logical connections how your statistic supports your claim.

Finally, don't make the mistake of leaving out the impact of the statistic on your audience. You must relate the statistic back to the individual lives of your audience members. Describe how the statistic would look if it were applied to them. If the statistic is "70% of people experience [insert consequence]," then tell your audience to "imagine that seven of the people in your row (assuming rows of ten), at random, struggled with [insert consequence]."

SHOCKING FACTS GRAB ATTENTION

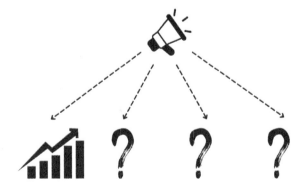

FIGURE 14: Hearing a piece of information we didn't know appeals to our desire for novelty; our desire to capture new

information. It suggests that your communication is valuable and worth paying attention to.

Historical Example: "Now, we have no better example of this than government's involvement in the farm economy over the last 30 years. Since 1955, the cost of this program has nearly doubled. One-fourth of farming in America is responsible for 85 percent of the farm surplus. Three-fourths of farming is out on the free market and has known a 21 percent increase in the per capita consumption of all its produce. You see, that one-fourth of farming that's regulated and controlled by the federal government. In the last three years we've spent 43 dollars in the feed grain program for every dollar bushel of corn we don't grow. [...] They've just declared Rice County, Kansas, a depressed area. Rice County, Kansas, has two hundred oil wells, and the 14,000 people there have over 30 million dollars on deposit in personal savings in their banks. And when the government tells you you're depressed, lie down and be depressed. [...] But the reverse is true. Each year the need grows greater; the program grows greater. We were told four years ago that 17 million people went to bed hungry each night. Well that was probably true. They were all on a diet. But now we're told that 9.3 million families in this country are poverty-stricken on the basis of earning less than 3,000 dollars a year. Welfare spending [is] 10 times greater than in the dark depths of the Depression. We're spending 45 billion dollars on welfare. Now do a little arithmetic, and you'll find that if we divided the 45 billion dollars up equally among those 9 million poor families, we'd be able to give each family 4,600 dollars a year. And this added to their present income should eliminate poverty. Direct aid to the poor, however, is only running only about 600 dollars per family. It would seem that someplace there must be some overhead." – Ronald Reagan

CREATE AN INFORMATION GAP

This technique captivates immediate attention. Find a common belief that isn't true. Poke a hole in that belief. Gain instant attention as people mentally scramble to fill their information gap.

Another approach is to find an important and relevant fact that most people don't know. Ask if they know it using the common "Did you know...?" statement. Experience immediate engagement as you overwhelm your audience with curiosity.

CURIOSITY GRABS ATTENTION

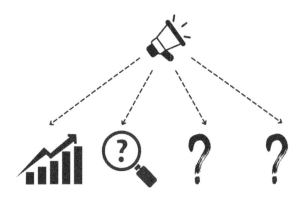

FIGURE 15: Curiosity is one of the most powerful impulses. In order to captivate the audience, present a gap between what they want to know and what they know, either by making them want to know something they don't know, or poking a hole in something they think they do.

Historical Example: "*If there is anyone out there who still doubts that America is a place where all things are possible; who still wonders if the dream of our founders is alive in our time; who still questions the power of our democracy, tonight is your answer.* It's the answer told by lines that stretched around schools and churches in numbers this nation has never seen; by people who waited three hours and four hours, many for the very first time in their lives, because they believed that this time must be different; that their voice could be that difference. It's the answer spoken by young and old, rich and poor, Democrat and Republican, black, white, Latino, Asian, Native American, gay, straight, disabled and not disabled – Americans who sent a message to the world that we have never been a collection of red states and blue states; we are, and always will be, the United States of America. It's the answer that led those who have been told for so long by so many to be cynical, and fearful, and doubtful of what we can achieve to put their hands on the arc of history and bend it once more toward the hope of a better day. It's been a long time coming, but tonight, because of what we did on this day, in this election, at this defining moment, change has come to America." – Barack Obama

---

KEY INSIGHT:

Ask Yourself This: What Would Your Audience Have to Hear In the First 15 Seconds to Listen to the Next 15 Minutes? What Would Have to Precede Your Message to Make Listening to Your Message Irresistible?

USE "SECRECY PHRASES"

Words are powerful, and more powerful than you know. Certain words have proven psychological effects on listeners. And secrecy phrases are some of those special words. What do they do? They build curiosity, and curiosity grabs attention. Here's the simple, step-by-step process of this strategy: Start your speech as you normally would. At the beginning, in the attention step, sprinkle "secrecy phrases." Then, if you prefer, take it a step further with "secrecy indicators."

Secrecy phrases are words that imply a big secret, like "little-known, hidden, veiled, unknown, forgotten, buried, etc."

Secrecy indicators are full sentences that imply a big secret. And when I found out this little-known secret, it challenged everything I thought I knew about [insert subject]." "Ever since I discovered this little-known problem, nothing was the same." "I'm going to let you all in on a hidden, little-known secret."

Secrecy indicators often contain secrecy phrases. They usually take this form: "when I found this secret, [positive outcome] happened." Say this without revealing the secret.

Want to make it even more unbearable for your audience? Want to make their curiosity much more visceral, and capture their attention as a result? String together a series of secrecy indicator sentences. Use plenty of secrecy phrases in them. Tease the world's most groundbreaking epiphany. And make sure the revelation is worth the hype.

KEY INSIGHT:

We Crave the Scarce, Secretive, Exclusive, and Little-Known.

LITTLE-KNOWN INFORMATION GRABS ATTENTION

FIGURE 16: We are wired to desire what is scarce and exclusive. This subtle, sneaky words signal a sense of scarcity to the subconscious mind.

ASK FOR A RAISE OF HANDS

Public speaking is often seen as one-way communication; as you, communicating to your audience, who is just receiving your communication. But asking for a raise of hands makes it two-way communication. And two-way communication is much more engaging than one-way communication. Raising a hand in response to a question is a form of communication, albeit very rudimentary communication. So ask your audience to raise their hands if, for example, they have ever been harmed by a problem relevant to your speech, they have any background in your subject area, they know a specific piece of information, or they experienced a relevant event.

But it's important that you also react to the poll. That solidifies the two-way communication paradigm (by immediately giving a response to their response to your request for a show of hands). It also tailors your speech to your specific audience (by adjusting the rest of your message to the information about the audience the poll revealed).

That's how you master the attention step. With four simple strategies, you can dramatically increase the attention (and thus the respect) you receive when you speak. These are the same techniques I have used in my long and fruitful career as a competitive public speaker. Use those four methods and you will have more attention, more applause, and more action.

TWO-WAY COMMUNICATION GRABS ATTENTION

FIGURE 17: The initiation of two-way communication grabs attention. Conversations are more engaging than listening to someone give a monologue.

THE NEED STEP: FOUR METHODS TO INSTANTLY CREATE A POWERFUL AUDIENCE NEED

Trying to influence people is trying to get them to move. And people move to escape pain or attain pleasure. This is why it is essential to express the potential pain caused by the unfilled need, as well as the pleasure attained by satisfying the need. The attention step is designed to grab attention for the remainder of the message, and though it is essential, the heart of the message begins here, with the need step.

APPEAL TO THE DESIRE TO IMPROVE

Human beings have a set of needs. Those needs are set in a hierarchy; in a pyramid. Abraham Maslow revealed his pyramidal framework of human motivation, and it is known as Maslow's Hierarchy of Needs. At the top of this pyramid of needs is the need to self-actualize: the need to improve, the need to grow, the need to fulfill potential, and the need to evolve.

To instantly make your audience see a need, use aspirational persuasion. Tell them what they could be. Show them how they have unfulfilled potential. Explain neglected areas of improvement in their lives. Don't do this in a judgmental way; do it with empathy, understanding, as someone who has been in their shoes, and as a trusted advisor. And above all, do it with tact and subtlety.

And remember: Don't talk about your solution just yet. That doesn't come until the satisfaction step. Right now, just focus on the need.

THE SELF-ACTUALIZATION IMPULSE CREATES NEED

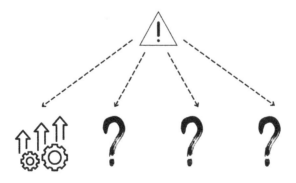

FIGURE 18: Humans have a desire to strive for our highest potential, both as individuals and collectively. It is said that tragedy is the gap between "what is" and "what could have

been." Appeal to our need for self-actualization by expressing "what could be."

Historical Example: "There is no strife, no prejudice, no national conflict in outer space as yet. Its hazards are hostile to us all. Its conquest deserves the best of all mankind, and its opportunity for peaceful cooperation many never come again. But why, some say, the moon? Why choose this as our goal? And they may well ask why climb the highest mountain? Why, 35 years ago, fly the Atlantic? Why does Rice play Texas? We choose to go to the moon. *We choose to go to the moon in this decade and do the other things, not because they are easy, but because they are hard, because that goal will serve to organize and measure the best of our energies and skills, because that challenge is one that we are willing to accept,* one we are unwilling to postpone, and one which we intend to win, and the others, too." – John F. Kennedy

APPEAL TO THE LIFE-FORCE EIGHT CORE DESIRES

Genetic evolution is a powerful force. And it has programmed into our brains eight core life-force desires: survival, enjoyment of life, life extension; enjoyment of food and beverages; freedom from fear, pain, and danger; sexual companionship; comfortable living conditions; to be superior, winning, keeping up with the Joneses; care and protection of loved ones; social approval.

There is a simple three-step process to applying this method. First, identify a life-force desire that connects to your speech. Second, show how it remains unfulfilled, or how it could be fulfilled to a greater degree, but do so tactfully. Do so implicitly, gently, and metaphorically. Repeatedly hit this pain-point of unfulfilled desire.

THE LIFE-FORCE EIGHT DESIRES CREATE NEED

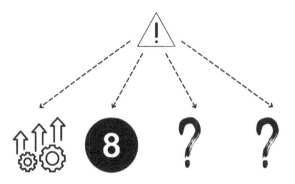

FIGURE 19: Appealing to the life-force eight desires creates need – this is a fundamental and inalienable aspect of our neurobiology.

Historical Example: "Poverty is a national problem, requiring improved national organization and support. But this attack, to be effective, must also be organized at the State and the local level and must be supported and directed by State and local efforts. For the war against poverty will not be won here in Washington. It must be won in the field, in every private home, in every public office, from the courthouse to the White House. The program I shall propose will emphasize this cooperative approach to help that one-fifth of all American families with incomes too small to even meet their basic needs. Our chief weapons in a more pinpointed attack will be better schools, and better health, and better homes, and better training, and better job opportunities to help more Americans, especially young Americans, escape from squalor and misery and unemployment rolls where other citizens help to carry them. Very often a lack of jobs and money is not the cause of poverty, but the symptom. The cause may lie deeper in our failure to give our fellow citizens a fair chance to develop their own capacities, in a lack of education and training, in a lack of medical care and housing, in a lack of decent communities in which to live and bring up their children. But whatever the cause, our joint Federal-local effort must pursue poverty, pursue it wherever it exists – in city slums and small towns, in sharecropper shacks or in migrant worker camps, on Indian Reservations, among whites as well as Negroes, among the young as well as the aged, in the boom towns and in the depressed areas. Our aim is not only to relieve the symptom of poverty, but to cure it and, above all, to prevent it. No single piece of legislation, however, is going to suffice." – Lyndon B. Johnson

---

KEY INSIGHT:

Inspirational Speech Must Speak to the Deepest Parts of Us.

The Archetypal Inspirational (And Influential) Message Is This: "Imagine What You Would Be If You Could Be Everything You Wanted to Be. You Have What It Takes to Actually Be That."

APPEAL TO EMOTION

Pathos is a rhetorical device proposed by Aristotle that has become a misunderstood buzzword. Most people misconstrue it as making your audience feel the "sad" emotions, like pity, for example. They are wrong. Pathos means making your audience feel whatever emotion will make them take action. In other words, pathos means achieving emotion-action convergence. Appeal to the emotion that matches your call to action. Want to make people solve a frustrating problem? Appeal to frustration, which is what the problem causes. Want to make people ready to face the future? Appeal to excitement and anticipation, which is what facing the future demands. Want to make people relaxed? Appeal to contentment, and satisfaction with the current state of things.

EMOTIONAL ENGAGEMENT PRODUCES NEED

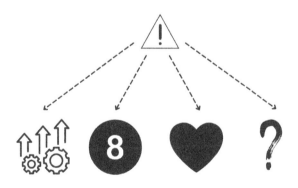

FIGURE 20: Appealing to emotion creates need, and creating a need activates an emotional response.

Historical Example: "Our streets will echo again with the laughter of our children, because no one will try to shoot them or sell them drugs anymore. Everyone who can work, will work, with today's permanent under class part of tomorrow's growing middle class. New miracles of medicine at last will reach not only those who can claim care now, but the children and hardworking families too long denied." – Bill Clinton

PAINT A TANTALIZING IMAGE OF THE FUTURE

Answer this question first: What does your audience want? Then, show them how the future can include that. Show them how the present doesn't. Paint in extreme detail this ideal future. Make the present seem lacking, and a need will develop. Figure out what your audience wants most, above all. Ask some of them in person and look for trends before you speak, or rely on your preexisting knowledge of your audience and human psychology. Connect this desire to your speech. Show them how the present is lacking this desire. Show the how the future can fulfill this desire. Emphasize the contrast between the lacking present and the abundant future.

A FUTURE-BASED CAUSE CREATES NEED

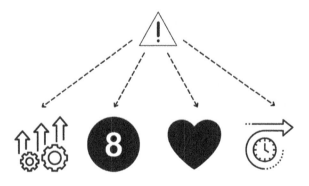

FIGURE 21: Create a need by presenting a positive vision for the future. Contrast this vision with the present.

Historical Example: "Your imagination, your initiative, and your indignation will determine whether we build a society where progress is the servant of our needs, or a society where old values and new visions are buried under unbridled growth. For in your time we have the opportunity to move not only toward the rich society and the powerful society, but upward to the Great Society. The Great Society rests on abundance and liberty for all. It demands an end to poverty and racial injustice, to which we are totally committed in our time. But that is just the beginning. The Great Society is a place where every child can find knowledge to enrich his mind and to enlarge his talents. It is a place where leisure is a welcome chance to build and reflect, not a feared cause of boredom and restlessness. It is a place where the city of man serves not only the needs of the body and the demands of commerce but the desire for beauty and the hunger for community. It is a place where man can renew contact with nature. It is a place which honors creation for its own sake and for what it adds to the understanding of the race. It is a place where men are more concerned with the quality of their goals than the quantity of their goods. But most of all, the Great Society is not a safe harbor, a resting place, a final objective, a finished work. It is a challenge constantly renewed, beckoning us toward a destiny where the meaning of our lives matches the marvelous products of our labor. So I want to talk to you today about three places where we begin to build the Great Society – in our cities, in our countryside, and in our classrooms." – Lyndon B. Johnson

THE SATISFACTION STEP: FOUR METHODS TO SATISFY THE AUDIENCE NEED

Problems and solutions are fundamental narrative elements of human reality, guiding our perceptions to conceive of the world in an understandable and useful way. We live in a world of problems and we seek to transform it into a world of solutions. While the problem-solution structure is a different technique we discuss in part two, the same basic principle of "what we have" versus "what we want to have" empowers the strength of the need and satisfaction steps.

DON'T TRY PITCHING UNTIL NOW

Don't try to pitch your solution until now. Why? Because it builds trust, context, and influence to postpone the pitch. If you are pitching an idea or a solution, it only makes sense in the context of a problem. Your solution only makes sense once you have established the need for it. First establishing the need and then presenting the solution makes the solution drastically more attractive. By keeping step two and step three distinct and separate, your audience sees that you aren't rushing to sell to them. This builds trust. It gives you time to build familiarity as a trusted advisor. This creates the strong impression that you care about them more than you care about getting their money (or whatever you want them to do).

POSTPONING THE PITCH OFFERS SATISFACTION

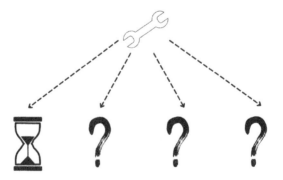

FIGURE 22: Delaying the satisfaction step offers satisfaction. Do not blur the steps. If you rush to pitch, you

lose trust and fail to lend a sense of necessity and urgency
to the solution you are advocating for.

USE "SAFETY WORDS"

Safety words are similar to secrecy phrases. If you sprinkle safety words in your satisfaction step, people believe it more on a subconscious level.

Here are some examples of safety words: "proven, verified, time-tested, expert-endorsed, scientifically-backed, evidenced, well-known," and the like. Compare these sentences: "And with this solution, you will gain at least 20% more profit per sale." "And with this proven, time-tested solution, you are guaranteed to gain at least 20% more profit per sale."

Adding words like "proven," "time-tested," and "guaranteed" makes it sound more psychologically convincing. The next method, personal safety indicators, steps it up a level.

CERTAINTY OFFERS SATISFACTION

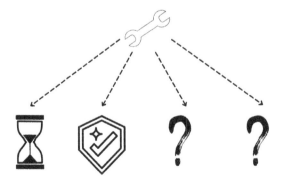

FIGURE 23: People only act in the presence of some measure of certainty that acting will produce their desired results.

USE PERSONAL "SAFETY INDICATORS"

Personal safety indicators are incredibly convincing sentences. "I was skeptical too. But when I tested this solution for myself, it worked as promised." It's that simple. Personal safety indicators are personal stories of how the solution worked for you (or another character – the only requirement is that the audience can identify with the character). By including these, you make your audience trust your solution more. You also build "audience relatability" by acknowledging your own skepticism.

TRUST OFFERS SATISFACTION

FIGURE 24: If you promise benefits but lack trust, the perceived benefit of acting how you propose remains zero.

Historical Example: "We must act today in order to preserve tomorrow. And let there be no misunderstanding – we are going to begin to act, beginning today. The economic ills we suffer have come upon us over several decades. They will not go away in days, weeks, or months, but they will go away. They will go away because we, as Americans, have the capacity now, as we have had in the past, to do whatever needs to be done to preserve this last and greatest bastion

of freedom. [...] *I do not believe in a fate that will all on us no matter what we do. I do believe in a fate that will fall on us if we do nothing.*"
– Ronald Reagan

APPLY THE RHETORICAL TRIANGLE

Pathos is using emotion. Logos is using logic. Ethos is using evidence. Of course, you should use all three. You already knew that. But most people lack the knowledge of how the three components interact: emotion convinces people, logic gives them a way to justify their emotional decisions, and ethos is the evidence used by logic. Start with ethos. Lay down your evidence, as well as reasons you are an authority on the subject (if this is appropriate). Then use logos to connect that evidence to pathos. Use pathos to gain persuasive power. In short, use logos (logic) to connect ethos (evidence) to pathos (the underlying emotional motivations to do something).

THE RHETORICAL TRIAD OFFERS SATISFACTION

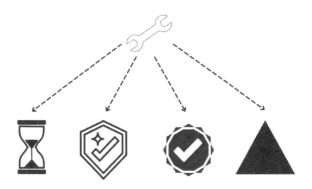

FIGURE 25: Apply Aristotle's 2,000-year-old framework of persuasion: ethos, pathos, and logos.

THE PROBLEM, AGITATE, SOLUTION, AGITATE STRUCTURE

STRUCTURE	"PASA" Structure			
BEHAVIORAL DUALITY	Escape		Approach	
SEMANTIC DUALITY	Problem		Solution	
EMOTIONAL DUALITY	Pain		Pleasure	
TEMPORAL DUALITY	Now		Later	
EXISTENTIAL DUALITY	Here		There	
DESIRE DUALITY	Aversion		Desire	
MODAL DUALITY	Chaos		Order	
STATE DUALITY	Actual		Potential	
KAIROS DUALITY	Conflict		Resolution	
THE SEQUENCE	**Problem**	**Agitate**	**Solution**	**Agitate**

KEY INSIGHT:

The Core Element of Compelling Speech Is a Problem.

Magnetic, Engaging, and Captivating Speech Aims to Wrestle with a Serious Problem.

The More Serious the Problem, the More Engaging the Speech.

THE VISUALIZATION STEP: HOW TO CREATE COMPELLING VISUALIZATIONS

We have six senses, not five. The "sixth sense" is the "mind's eye." It is our ability to create and observe visualizations in our minds; unseen visual experiences that are undoubtedly "sensed," even if they are conjured up by your own mind, in your own mind, at will.

USE POWERFUL VISUAL ADJECTIVES

Do you want to make your audience see things? You can. Use powerful visual adjectives (PVAs). They will see what you' are describing in their minds. If you go up to an audience and say "sunset," they can't help but see a sunset in their minds. But "sunset" isn't a PVA. It isn't even an adjective.

PVAs must represent a distinct aspect of the noun to which you attach them. They must be detail oriented, and focused on the small details of the noun. They must be concrete, revealing something physically visible. "Striking" is not concrete. "Orange" is. They must be evocative; they must be focused on evoking a visceral emotional reaction. And lastly, the must be open, not so specific that the audience can't "fill in the blanks" to their individual content.

Here are some PVAs you can apply to "sunset" that fulfill those requirements: "orange," "bright," "shimmering."

Here are some PVAs that are not powerful. They are just "visual adjectives," and don't work the same way: "colorful," "beautiful," "striking." These are not specific, concrete, or detail oriented.

"Orange, bright, shimmering sunset" paints a distinct mental image. "Colorful, beautiful, striking sunset" does not.

PVA-SATURATED LANGUAGE INSPIRES VISUALIZATION

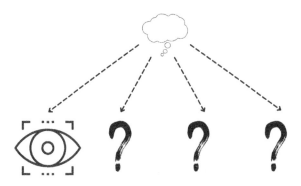

FIGURE 26: Powerful visual adjectives inspire visualization by beaming themselves into our psyches. But remember that not all visual adjectives are powerful.

Historical Example: "And that's about all I have to say tonight, except for one thing. The past few days when I've been at that window upstairs, I've thought a bit of the '*shining city upon a hill.*' The phrase comes from John Winthrop, who wrote it to describe the America he imagined. What he imagined was important because he was an early Pilgrim, an early freedom man. He journeyed here on what today we'd call *a little wooden boat,* and like the other Pilgrims, he was looking for a home that would be free. I've spoken of *the shining city* all my political life, but I don't know if I ever quite communicated what I saw when I said it. But in my mind it was *a tall, proud city built on rocks stronger than oceans, windswept,* God-blessed, and teeming with people of all kinds living in harmony and peace; a city with *free ports that hummed with commerce and creativity.* And if there had to be city walls, the walls had doors and the doors were open to anyone with the will and the heart to get here. That's how I saw it, and see it still. And how stands the city on this winter night? More prosperous, more secure, and happier than it was 8 years ago. But more than that: After 200 years, two centuries, she still stands strong and true on the *granite ridge, and her glow* has held steady no matter what storm. And she's *still a beacon, still a magnet* for all who must have freedom, for all the pilgrims from all the lost places who are *hurtling through the darkness*, toward home. [...] Watching on television these last few nights I've seen also the warmth with which you greeted Nancy and you also filled my heart with joy when you did that. May I say some words. There are cynics who say that a party platform is something that no one bothers to read and is doesn't very often amount to much. Whether it is different this time than it has ever been before, I believe the Republican party has a platform that is *a banner of bold, unmistakable colors with no pale pastel shades.* We have just heard a call to arms, based on that platform." – Ronald Reagan

ENGAGING THE VAKOG SENSES

These are the commonly-cited five senses. V: visual A: auditory K: kinesthetic (feeling of body). O: olfactory. G: gustatory. With a simple process, you can successfully engage all of these senses.

Decide on a clear visualization of the future outcome. It can be symbolic. Paint a mental movie in your audience's mind of this future. Use each of the VAKOG senses (or whichever ones are appropriate and fitting) to paint this mental movie. To make this process more natural, you can tell a story that touches on the senses.

Like PVAs, when you use the VAKOG senses to paint a mental movie, your audience can't help getting entrapped in it.

DESCRIBING VIVID SCENES INSPIRES VISUALIZATION

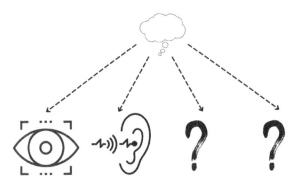

FIGURE 27: Engaging the VAKOG senses more broadly creates an even more tantalizing visualization.

Historical Example: "From this joyful *mountaintop* of celebration, we *hear* a *call* to service in the *valley*. We have *heard* the *trumpets*. We have changed the *guard*. And now, each in our way, and with God's help, we must answer the *call*." – Bill Clinton

TAP INTO AUDIENCE IMAGINATION ("IMAGINE...")

Imagination is the single most powerful component of persuasion. You either tap into imagination and persuade or don't and fail to influence.

Which will it be? The first one, I hope. All you have to do is say "Imagine [benefit one], [benefit two], [benefit three]."

Command them to imagine, and they will imagine. They can't refuse. Psychologically, they can't. They will imagine what you want them to imagine, no matter how hard they try not to. It is so irresistible because it is how we interpret language: we understand a sentence by imagining it.

APPEALING TO IMAGINATION INSPIRES VISUALIZATION

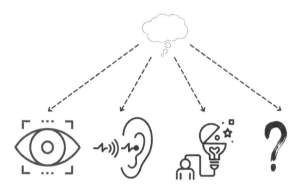

FIGURE 28: "Imagine" is one of the most powerful words in the English language.

Historical Example: "And then as I tried to write – *let your own minds turn to that task.* You're going to write for people a hundred years from now who know all about us, we know nothing about them. We don't know what kind of world they'll be living in. And suddenly I thought to myself, If I write of the problems, they'll be the domestic problems of which the President spoke here tonight; the challenges confronting us, the erosion of freedom taken place under Democratic rule in this country, the invasion of private rights, the controls and restrictions on the vitality of the great free economy that we enjoy. These are the challenges that we must meet and then again there is that challenge of which he spoke that we live in a world in which the great powers have aimed and poised at each other horrible missiles of destruction, nuclear weapons that can in a matter of minutes arrive at each other's country and destroy virtually the civilized world we live in." – Ronald Reagan

EMPOWER POSITIVE COUNTERFACTUAL SIMULATION

When your audience inevitably imagines the two principle paths (I'll explain), they will go through counterfactual simulation (I'll explain) and it must be positive (I'll explain).

Principle path one: "what happens if I do what this speaker wants me to do? Principle path two: "what happens if I don't do what this speaker wants me to do?" Counterfactual simulation: imagining the future consequences of present actions to make a decision. Positive counterfactual simulation: imagining the future consequences of path one to be positive (and of path two to be negative).

This is the framework you must understand in order to ace this step. Your audience must imagine that doing what you want them to do will yield massive positive consequences. But of equal importance is this: They must imagine that not doing what you want them to do will yield negative consequences. Thus, they must perceive that doing what you want will help them attain benefits and avoid losses.

COUNTERFACTUAL SIMULATION INSPIRES VISUALIZATION

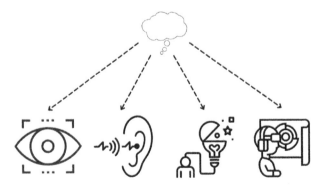

FIGURE 29: Create a dynamic in which your audience only predicts positive outcomes from acting how you want them to act, and they will act how you want them to act.

Historical Example: "I have, myself, full confidence that if all do their duty, if nothing is neglected, and if the best arrangements are made, as they are being made, *we shall prove ourselves once again able to defend our Island home, to ride out the storm of war, and to outlive the menace of tyranny, if necessary for years, if necessary alone.* At any rate, that is what we are going to try to do. That is the resolve of His Majesty's Government-every man of them. That is the will of Parliament and the nation. The British Empire and the French Republic, linked together in their cause and in their need, will defend to the death their native soil, aiding each other like good comrades to the utmost of their strength. Even though large tracts of Europe and many old and famous States have fallen or may fall into the grip of the Gestapo and all the odious apparatus of Nazi rule, *we shall not flag or fail. We shall go on to the end,* we shall fight in France, we shall fight on the seas and oceans, we shall fight with growing confidence and growing strength in the air, we shall defend our Island, whatever the cost may be, we shall fight on the beaches, we shall fight on the landing grounds, we shall fight in the fields and in the streets, we shall fight in the hills; *we shall never surrender, and even if, which I do not for a moment believe, this Island or a large part of it were subjugated and starving, then our Empire beyond the seas, armed and guarded by the British Fleet, would carry on the struggle, until, in God's good time, the New World, with all its power and might, steps forth to the rescue and the liberation of the old.*" – Winston Churchill

THE ACTION STEP: FOUR PROVEN METHODS TO INSPIRE FAST AND ENTHUSIASTIC ACTION

This is what it all comes down to. This is what it's all about. This is where you call your audience to action. Now, if they don't take the action, does it mean you failed? No, because there is a spectrum of persuasive success. On the most successful end is every member of your audience doing exactly what you want them to do in exactly the way you want them to do it (and when). This rarely occurs. On the least successful end is every member of your audience doing the exact opposite of what you want them to do. Somewhere in the middle, toward the successful end, is a more realistic goal: getting some people to follow through enthusiastically, leaving behind a small handful of stragglers, but getting most people to subtly change their belief-patterns in favor of your position, or to take a more moderate action toward the general end you advocate. In some instances, like sales, you want complete commitment. In other persuasive scenarios, remember the spectrum of persuasion.

KEY INSIGHT:

If You Persuaded Complete Agreement, You Won.

You Also Won If They Even Considered Your Point, If You Opened Their Eyes To a New Perspective, And If You Nudged Them Even One Degree Over.

STRONG ACTION VERBS

Want to get your audience to take action? Strong action verbs are exactly how you inspire action. Strong action verbs motivate people, inspire people, and direct people. And guess what you need to receive action? Motivated, inspired people, directed toward a certain action.

Here are some examples of strong action verbs: "Get [benefit]." "Make [improvement]." "Start [process]." "Seize [opportunity]." "Go [action]." They are crisp, compelling, and commanding. They are clear. They precede the "hard" call to action; that is, the most desirable action you want your audience members to take. They are not always appropriate, but particularly in situations calling for inspiration – that is, motivation – they are highly effective, and have been used in the legendary speeches of legendary leaders for centuries. They are a direct call; a clear request to affirm or deny. They are bold and confident.

STRONG ACTION-ORIENTED LANGUAGE GETS ACTION

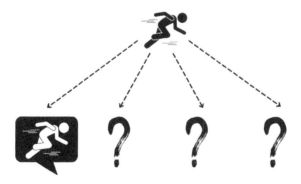

FIGURE 30: Strong action verbs are clear, unequivocal, unambiguous, and bold tools for motivating action – once you have applied the rest of the structure, of course.

Historical Example: "In the long history of the world, only a few generations have been granted the role of defending freedom in its hour of maximum danger. I do not shrink from this responsibility – I welcome it. I do not believe that any of us would exchange places with any other people or any other generation. The energy, the faith, the devotion which we bring to this endeavor will light our country and all who serve it – and the glow from that fire can truly light the world. And so, my fellow Americans: *ask* not what your country can do for you – *ask* what you can do for your country. My fellow citizens of the world: *ask* not what America will do for you, but what together we can do for the freedom of man. Finally, whether you are citizens of America or citizens of the world, *ask* of us here the same high standards of strength and sacrifice which we *ask* of you. With a good conscience our only sure reward, with history the final judge of our deeds, let us go forth to lead the land we love, *asking* His blessing and His help, but knowing that here on earth God's work must truly be our own." – John F. Kennedy

TANGIBLE TAKEAWAYS

People are busy. Just think about your own life. Busy, right? So, people forget, even if they are motivated, inspired, and directed. How do you make people remember your call to action? Give them a tangible takeaway. This will be a physical reminder in their home or office; an extension of you, telling them to take action. For example, a short, printed packet summarizing your message and directing them to action achieves this purpose.

TANGIBLE TAKEAWAYS GET ACTION

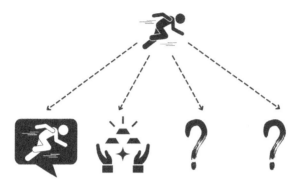

FIGURE 31: Tangible takeaways replicate you and allow you to follow around your audience members when they go home (unless they decide to throw the mini-you in the trash can – who knows?)

REASONABLE CALL TO ACTION

People hate change. People are inert. People have habit loops so strong that they last for their entire lives. This is part of why it is so hard to motivate action. But if you make the action reasonable, the chances of your audience members following through rises.

Would you rather propose an extreme action and have nobody do it? Or propose a reasonable action and have 50% of your audience do it?

KEY INSIGHT:

A Good Reality Is Often Worth More Than a Great Promise.

REASONABLE CALLS TO ACTION GET ACTION

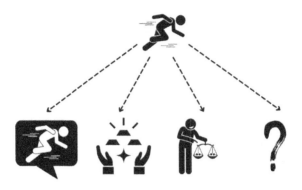

FIGURE 32: Is what you are calling your audience to do something you are willing to do yourself?

TACK ONTO EXISTING HABIT STRUCTURES

People live their lives through habit structures. And to get action, perhaps for decades, you must do these two things: first, tack action onto existing habit structures; second, make your proposed action a habit-loop.

Connect your action to an existing habit. Want people to read a section of the daily news every day? Connect that to an existing habit structure, like morning coffee. The habit structure you connect to your action must be a structure that most of your audience has, a structure that occurs frequently, and a structure that allows for multitasking.

Here's what a habit-loop looks like: You must provide a psychological queue (like bedtime). You must provide a process (like tooth-brushing). You must provide a reward for that process (like teeth that feel clean and the nice feeling of the foamy tooth-paste). Supply these ingredients to your audience members. "Remember when you see politicians say they support policy X (psychological queue) to ask yourself with the second- and third-order consequences of X are (process), and you will come to learn the truth of what they really want to do if they attain power (reward)."

HABIT STRUCTURES GET ACTION

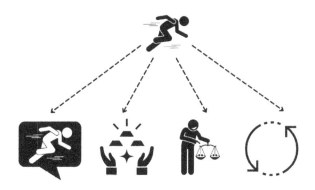

FIGURE 33: Habit structures create the vast majority of the actions we take. Reverse-engineer them to your advantage.

MONROE'S MOTIVATED SEQUENCE REVISITED

FIGURE 34: We will shortly discuss proven and advanced persuasive methods to layer upon this structure.

HOW TO GRAB ATTENTION

FIGURE 35: Reveal a shocking statistic, appeal to curiosity, tease little-known information, and create two-way communication.

HOW TO CREATE A NEED

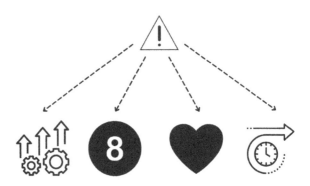

FIGURE 36: Appeal to the self-actualization impulse, the life-force eight desires, emotion, and present a future-based cause.

HOW TO OFFER SATISFACTION

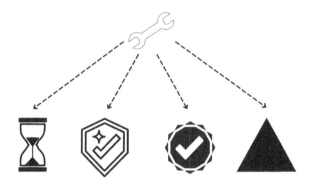

FIGURE 37: Postpone the pitch, apply safety-indicating words, present personal safety-indicators, and use ethos, pathos, and logos.

HOW TO INSPIRE VISUALIZATION

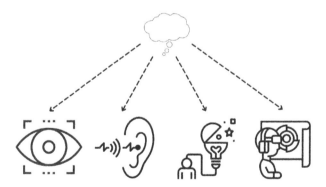

FIGURE 38: Use powerful visual adjectives, the VAKOG senses, the "imagine" phrase, and empower positive counterfactual simulations.

HOW TO GET ACTION

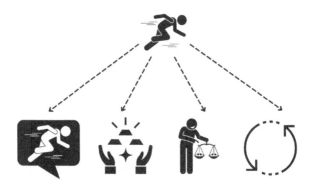

FIGURE 39: Use strong action verbs, offer a tangible takeaway, present a reasonable call to action, and graft your proposed action onto the audience's preexisting habit loops, tapping into their power to motivate action.

KEY INSIGHT:

Your Rhetorical Toolbox Is Just That: A Toolbox. Sometimes, One Tool Is All You Need. Other Times, You Need to Use Many Together. And Often, the Wrong Tool Won't Get the Job Done.

A SECRET METHOD FOR ADAPTING MONROE'S MOTIVATED SEQUENCE

A little-known strategy adapts Monroe's Motivated Sequence, allowing you to gain total, undivided attention from your audiences (even when you aren't trying to persuade). This method allows you to completely rework Monroe's Motivated Sequence to any situation – even those that are not primarily persuasive.

The strategy is called The Informational Motivated Sequence. While Monroe's Motivated Sequence is designed for persuasive speeches, it can be adapted for informational speeches with this process. In this case, the motivated sequence takes up significantly less time. For a persuasive speech, Monroe's Motivated Sequence is the entire speech. For an informational speech however, the motivated sequence is shorter and is motivates the following action: listening to you.

Here's how a 15-minute persuasive speech could be structured with Monroe's motivated sequence: Attention (3 minutes). Need (3 minutes). Satisfaction (3 minutes). Visualization (3 minutes). Action (3 minutes).

Here's how an informational speech of roughly the same length can be structured with the informational motivated sequence: Attention (1-minute maximum). Need (1-minute maximum). Satisfaction (1-minute maximum). Visualization (1-minute maximum). Information (10 minutes minimum). Action (1-minute maximum, if applicable)

During the attention step of the informational motivated sequence, you should get your audience's attention. In this case, do so in a way that gradually moves them into the information.

In the need step, you should clearly show your audience an area of knowledge that they need to capture; show them a gap between "the knowledge they have" and "the knowledge they need," and crucially, expose the consequences of this gap. Tell them why they should listen, and show them what need your information fulfills. Clearly establish why your information is worth their time. Connect it to their wants and desires. Connect it to their lives. Think of a problem that arises out of not knowing the information you are about to give them, and describe it. Describe the impacts of not knowing what you are about to say.

In the satisfaction step, clearly explain why the information you are going to give them solves the problem or fulfills a need that they have. Present your information as the solution to one of their most difficult, frustrating problems.

In the visualization step, show your audience what life will be like once they understand your information. Perhaps you are speaking to businesspeople who don't understand a crucial business process. Show them how wonderful it will feel to know that business process inside and out.

The information step is, of course, the most crucial. In a persuasive speech, you are trying to convince your audience to take up a certain solution, perform an action, or purchase something. Thus, the entirety of the speech should suit that purpose. With the informational motivated sequence, however, your main purpose is still to inform. The informational motivated sequence is essentially condensing Monroe's Motivated Sequence and putting it in front of an informational speech. The main focus is still informing.

Note that the in the Informational Motivated Sequence, the timeframe is ten minutes minimum for the information, and a maximum of four minutes for the first four steps of the motivated sequence. On the contrary, in Monroe's Motivated Sequence for persuasive speeches, each step of the sequence gets three minutes.

Lastly, in the action step, tell your audience what to do with your information. Once again, with the example of explaining a crucial business process to unknowing businesspeople, tell them the first point in their organizations where they can begin applying your information. Or if you prefer, tell them how to continue learning more about the area of knowledge.

This brings us to the end of our discussion of Monroe's Motivated Sequence. Now, we turn to discussing advanced, little-known theories of influential communication. Monroe's Motivated Sequence is the foundation; you stack the strategies revealed in part two on top of it, although they can be used independently.

THE INFORMATIONAL MOTIVATED SEQUENCE VISUALIZED

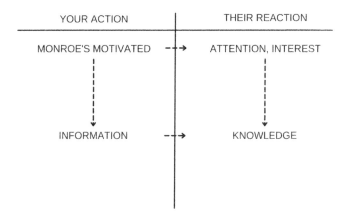

FIGURE 40: Squish Monroe's Motivated Sequence to get attention and build interest before an informational speech – use it as an opener – and then continue with the speech to convey the knowledge you wish to impart.

...................................Chapter Summary...................................

- The first step of Monroe's Motivated Sequence is to capture attention. Without capturing attention, you can't influence.
- The second step of Monroe's Motivated Sequence is to present a need. Why do people need what you're offering?
- The third step of Monroe's Motivated Sequence is to present a way to satisfy the need: your solution or proposal.

- The fourth step of Monroe's Motivated Sequence is to help the audience visualize the satisfaction of their need.
- The fifth step of Monroe's Motivated Sequence is to present the action they should take.
- This is the foundational framework of influence. The advanced strategies revealed in part two build upon it.

KEY INSIGHT:

If You Seek to Influence, Then Influence. If You Seek to Inform, You Must Still Influence.

You Must Influence Them to Care About Your Information.

Don't Let Them Wonder Why It Matters, Why It Helps Them, And Why It's Worthwhile.

Tell Them Clearly.

THE STRUCTURE AND THE STRATEGIES (PART ONE)

1	Monroe's Motivated Sequence
1.1	Apply Monroe's Motivated Sequence
1.2	Attention, Need, Satisfaction, Visualization, Action
1.3	Grab Attention as a Prerequisite to Influence and Persuasion
1.4	Present a Need to Validate Your Proposal or Solution
1.5	Offer the Satisfaction of the Need to Motivate Action
1.6	Present a Visualization of the Satisfaction to Raise Desire
1.7	Convey the Action that Will Move Them Toward Satisfaction
1.8	To Earn Attention, Use a Statistic
1.9	To Earn Attention, Create an Information Gap
1.10	To Earn Attention, Use "Secrecy Phrases"
1.11	To Earn Attention, Ask for a Raise of Hands
1.12	To Present a Need, Appeal to the Desire to Improve
1.13	To Present a Need, Appeal to the Life-Force Eight Core Desires
1.14	To Present a Need, Appeal to Emotion
1.15	To Present a Need, Paint a Tantalizing Image of the Future
1.16	To Offer Satisfaction, Don't Pitch Until Now
1.17	To Offer Satisfaction, Use "Safety Words"
1.18	To Offer Satisfaction, Use Personal "Safety Indicators"
1.19	To Offer Satisfaction, Apply the Rhetorical Triangle

1.20	To Create Visualization, Present Powerful Visual Adjectives
1.21	To Create Visualization, Engage the VAKOG Senses
1.22	To Create Visualization, Tap into Audience Imagination
1.23	To Create Visualization, Empower Positive Counterfactuals
1.24	To Motivate Action, Use Strong Action Verbs
1.25	To Motivate Action, Offer Tangible Takeaways
1.26	To Motivate Action, Present a Reasonable Call to Action
1.27	To Motivate Action, Tack onto Existing Habit Structures
1.28	Apply the Informational Motivated Sequence
1.29	Squish Monroe's Motivated Sequence
1.30	Place Monroe's in Front of an Informational Speech
1.31	Convey the Value of the Information and Hold Attention
2	**The Advanced Strategies**

Email Peter D. Andrei, the author of the Speak for Success collection and the President of Speak Truth Well LLC directly.

pandreibusiness@gmail.com

USING MONROE'S MOTIVATED SEQUENCE AS A SUBSTRUCTURE OF A THREE-POINT SPEECH

"A decade ago, we had a government that worked. Now, our government is badly broken."

"To fix our country, we need to do [action one], [action two], and [action three]."

""So, by [action one], [action two] and [action three], we can fix our government and restore our country."

Claim These Free Resources that Will Help You Unleash the Power of Your Words and Speak with Confidence. Visit www.speakforsuccesshub.com/toolkit for Access.

18 Free PDF Resources

12 Iron Rules for Captivating Story, 21 Speeches that Changed the World, 341-Point Influence Checklist, 143 Persuasive Cognitive Biases, 17 Ways to Think On Your Feet, 18 Lies About Speaking Well, 137 Deadly Logical Fallacies, 12 Iron Rules For Captivating Slides, 371 Words that Persuade, 63 Truths of Speaking Well, 27 Laws of Empathy, 21 Secrets of Legendary Speeches, 19 Scripts that Persuade, 12 Iron Rules For Captivating Speech, 33 Laws of Charisma, 11 Influence Formulas, 219-Point Speech-Writing Checklist, 21 Eloquence Formulas

Claim These Free Resources that Will Help You Unleash the Power of Your Words and Speak with Confidence. Visit www.speakforsuccesshub.com/toolkit for Access.

30 Free Video Lessons

We'll send you one free video lesson every day for 30 days, written and recorded by Peter D. Andrei. Days 1-10 cover authenticity, the prerequisite to confidence and persuasive power. Days 11-20 cover building self-belief and defeating communication anxiety. Days 21-30 cover how to speak with impact and influence, ensuring your words change minds instead of falling flat. Authenticity, self-belief, and impact – this course helps you master three components of confidence, turning even the most high-stakes presentations from obstacles into opportunities.

Claim These Free Resources that Will Help You Unleash the Power of Your Words and Speak with Confidence. Visit www.speakforsuccesshub.com/toolkit for Access.

2 Free Workbooks

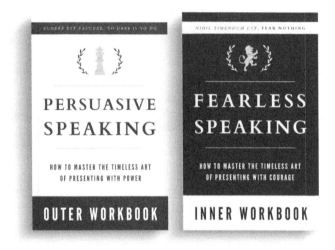

We'll send you two free workbooks, including long-lost excerpts by Dale Carnegie, the mega-bestselling author of *How to Win Friends and Influence People* (5,000,000 copies sold). *Fearless Speaking* guides you in the proven principles of mastering your inner game as a speaker. *Persuasive Speaking* guides you in the time-tested tactics of mastering your outer game by maximizing the power of your words. All of these resources complement the Speak for Success collection.

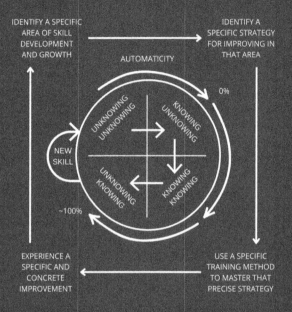

How do anxious speakers turn into articulate masters of the
craft? Here's how: With the bulletproof, scientifically-proven,
2,500-year-old (but mostly forgotten) process pictured above.

First, we identify a specific area of improvement. Perhaps
your body language weakens your connection with the
audience. At this point, you experience "unknowing
unknowing." You don't know you don't know the strategy you
will soon learn for improving in this area.

Second, we choose a specific strategy for improving in this
area. Perhaps we choose "open gestures," a type of
gesturing that draws the audience in and holds attention.

At this point, you experience "knowing unknowing." You know you don't know the strategy. Your automaticity, or how automatically you perform the strategy when speaking, is 0%.

Third, we choose a specific drill or training method to help you practice open gestures. Perhaps you give practice speeches and perform the gestures. At this point, you experience "knowing knowing." You know you know the strategy.

And through practice, you formed a weak habit, so your automaticity is somewhere between 0% and 100%.

Fourth, you continue practicing the technique. You shift into "unknowing knowing." You forgot you use this type of gesture, because it became a matter of automatic habit. Your automaticity is 100%.

And just like that, you've experienced a significant and concrete improvement. You've left behind a weakness in communication and gained a strength. Forever. Every time you speak, you use this type of gesture, and you do it without even thinking about it. This alone can make the difference between a successful and unsuccessful speech.

Now repeat. Master a new skill. Create a new habit. Improve in a new area. How else could we improve your body language? What about the structure of your communication? Your persuasive strategy? Your debate skill? Your vocal modulation? With this process, people gain measurable and significant improvements in as little as one hour. Imagine if you stuck with it over time. This is the path to mastery. This is the path to unleashing the power of your words.

Access your 18 free PDF resources, 30 free video lessons, and 2 free workbooks from this link: www.speakforsuccesshub.com/toolkit

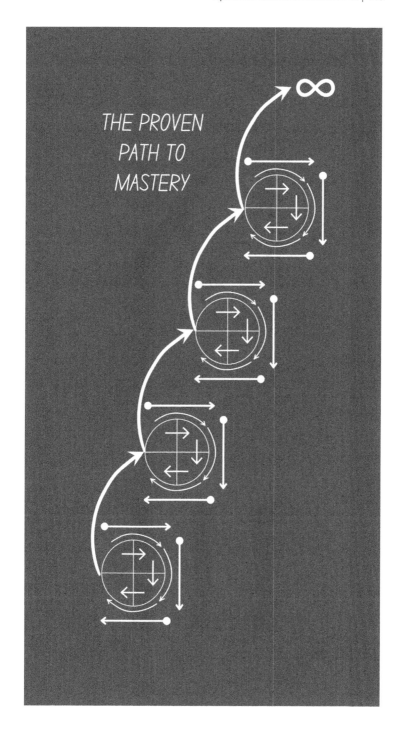

THE PROVEN
PATH TO
MASTERY

SPEAK FOR SUCCESS COLLECTION BOOK

INFLUENCE CHAPTER

THE STRATEGIES:
The Little-Known Secrets of Advanced Influence

ADVANCED INFLUENCE

W HILE 99% OF PEOPLE YOU ENCOUNTER in your career will not know what you learned up until now, I want you to consider that background. This final section breaks open the safe of communication theory. Nobody knows all of what I'm about to show you. They might know some, but not all, and most won't know any. You will learn the secrets that define the inner-fabric of effective communication; you will learn the secrets known only by the world's best communicators, who use these strategies to own the stage with ease, influence with subtle strategy, and speak with complete confidence. These strategies stack on top of the structure.

THE TRIFOLD EQUATION THEORY OF COMMUNICATION

Instantly become three times as powerful when you speak.

What if I told you that three equations – yes, three mathematical equations – defined good communication? What if I told you that if you want to master effective communication, all you have to do is apply these equations and engineer your words to maximize their mathematical values? What if I told you that practice would allow you to do this by default, without having to expend any effort?

These equations came to me when I was analyzing the most effective political and business speeches of all time. I realized that underlying thread of commonality was the satisfaction of these equations. The equations address substance, sentiment, and rhetoric. Let's start with substance.

THE THREE EQUATIONS OF INFLUENCE

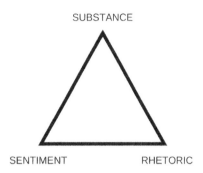

FIGURE 41: You can boil down much of effective influence to substance, sentiment, and rhetoric, and the three equations we use to measure them.

SUBSTANCE

I'm going to present to you a quasi-equation: Substance = Information / Words. If you want to increase the substance of your speech, find a way to pack more information into fewer words.

There are two key lessons relating to substance that can be drawn from the world of politics. Firstly, politicians have an astounding ability to, given the right circumstances, pack an incredible amount of information into very few words. Secondly, politicians also have an astounding ability to, given the wrong circumstances, pack very little information into an incredible number of words. Politicians have developed a reputation for being on the wrong end of the "substance = information / words" equation. But they can frequently be on the right side of that equation as well.

It's very difficult to quantify information transferred in a speech. For the purposes of this example, every time a politician makes a complete statement or presents a complete idea, they will gain one "information point." They will gain half a point when they present information that is contextual or tangential but still relevant. They will also gain half a point when they first repeat an idea they already gained a point for, and zero points for further repetitions. Lastly, they will gain half a point when they make introductory statements. This is less straightforward than it seems given the frequent use of emotive, implicative, and evocative language that condenses even more information in fewer words.

First, let's begin with an example of a highly substantive statement from a man named Ben Sasse, a senator from Nebraska who is a self-proclaimed independent that caucuses with one of the major parties. He was making a statement in critique of the functions of Congress, which was delivered on September 4, 2018:

"[of the current state of congress] How did we get here, and how do we fix it? [+0.5 introductory] I want to make just four brief points [+0.5 introductory]. Number one: in our system, the legislative branch is supposed to be the center of our politics [+1]. Number two: it's not [+1]. Why not? Because for the last century [+0.5 contextual], and increasing by the decade right now [+0.5 contextual], more and more legislative authority is delegated to the executive branch every year [+1]. Both parties do it [+1]. The legislature is impotent [+1]. The legislature is weak [+0.5 repetitive]. And most people here want their jobs more than they really want to do legislative work [+1], and so they punt most of the work to the next branch [+1]. The third consequence is that this transfer of power means the people yearn for a place where politics can actually be done [+1], and when we don't do a lot of big actual political debating here [+0.5 contextual], we transfer it to the Supreme Court [+1], and that's why the supreme court is increasingly a substitute political battleground in America [+1]. It is not healthy [+1], but it is what happens and it's something that our founders wouldn't be able to make any sense of [+1]. And fourth and finally: we badly need to restore the proper duties and the balance of power from our constitutional system [+1]."

So, let's calculate his substance score. This statement was 204 words total, and Ben Sasse earned an impressive 16 information points. 16 / 204 = a substance score of 0.078. This is a very good score.

Now, let's compare this to another statement, this time given by former president Jimmy Carter in a debate against incumbent Gerald Ford on October 22, 1976:

"Well I might say first of all that I think in case of the Carter administration the sacrifices would be much less [+1]. Mr. Ford's own uh – environmental agency has projected a 10 percent unemployment rate by 1978 [+1] if he's uh – president [+0.5 contextual]. The American people are ready to make sacrifices if they are part of the process [+1]. If they know that they will be helping to make decisions and won't be excluded from being an involved party to the national purpose [+0.5 repetitive]. The major effort we must put forward is to put our people back to work [+1]. And I think that this uh – is one example where uh – a lot of people have selfish, grasping ideas now [+1]. I remember 1973 in the depth of the uh – energy crisis [+0.5 contextual] when President Nixon called on the American people to make a sacrifice [+0.5 contextual], to cut down on the waste of uh – gasoline, to cut down on the uh – speed of automobiles [+1]. It was a – a tremendous surge of patriotism, that "I want to make a sacrifice for my country [+1]." I think we uh – could call together, with strong leadership in the White House [+0.5 contextual], business, industry and labor, and say let's have voluntary price restraints [+1]. Let's lay down some guidelines so we don't have continuing inflation [+0.5 repetitive]. We can also have a – an end to the extremes. We now have one extreme for instance, of some welfare recipients, who by taking advantage of the welfare laws, the housing laws, the uh – Medicaid uh – laws, and the uh – food stamp laws, make over $10 thousand a year [+1] and uh – they don't have to pay any taxes on it [+1]. At the other extreme, uh – just 1 percent of the richest people in our country derive 25 percent of all the tax benefits

[+1]. So both those extremes grasp for advantage [+1] and the person who has to pay that expense is the middle-income family [+1] who's still working for a living and they have to pay for the rich who have privilege [+0.5 repetitive], and for the poor who are not working [+0.5 repetitive]. But I think uh – uh – a balanced approach, with everybody being part of it and a striving for unselfishness [+1], could help as it did in 1973 to let people sacrifice for their own country [+1]. I know I'm ready for it. I think the American people are too."

Jimmy Carter earned 19 information points over the course of 385 words, earning him a substance score of 19 / 385, which equals 0.049. This is still a very good score, but not as good as Ben Sasse's impressive 0.078.

If it helps make substance scores more intuitive, you can multiply them by a factor of 100. 0.078 becomes 7.8, and 0.049 becomes 4.9. This doesn't change anything aside from making the numbers more intuitive.

What specifically makes Ben Sasse's statement so substantive? What strategies did he use to earn a score of 0.078? He said extremely succinct phrases, such as "Both parties do it [+1]. The legislature is impotent [+1]." Those two sentences alone have a substance score of 0.25. Eight words deliver two complete ideas. Additionally, he presented pieces of consecutive contextual information, as seen when he said "Because for the last century [+0.5 contextual], and increasing by the decade right now [+0.5 contextual], more and more legislative authority is delegated to the executive branch every year [+1]." Furthermore, he used very little repetition, making only one repetitive point. Repetition isn't a bad thing. On the contrary, it can be beneficial. It doesn't do much for substance score, however. Especially when the ideas in a speech are presented as clearly as they were in this segment of Ben Sasse's statement, there's no need for repetition. Lastly, Ben Sasse also presented his information in a very logical way, by listing his main points: "Number one [...] Number two

[...] The third consequence [...] and fourth and finally." This strategy not only makes the information easier to grasp and understand cohesively, but increases substance score by preventing words from being spent on transitions.

Using these methods to maximize the substance of your speech is helpful if it's a speech solely designed to inform. Some scenarios require a little more finesse, but these strategies are still extremely powerful. In some scenarios, style is king. In other scenarios, however, efficiency is king, and it is a style in and of itself.

There is a French phrase called "langue de bois," which roughly translates to "language of the woods" because it serves to obscure rather than clarify a message. This phrase has been used to characterize a type of empty, meaningless language that is full of ambiguity and is incredibly vague. The closest phrases we have in English are "empty talk" and "wooden language."

Avoid "langue de bois" at all costs. Politicians have been forced to adapt and learn how to maximize substance when speaking with no preparation. This is a skill that comes only with practice, and can be difficult at first. However, it's fairly easy to maximize substance when writing and memorizing a speech. In this scenario, you have the benefit of being able to rewrite, rephrase, and reshape your speech in order to maximize the value of the substance equation.

You shouldn't immediately aim to increase your substance score. Some situations demand a more moderate balance between substance and style, although there is a "no-nonsense" style associated with highly substantive statements like the one made by Ben Sasse.

THE SUBSTANCE EQUATION

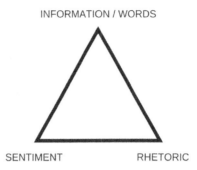

FIGURE 42: Raise your substance by raising the amount of information you convey per word.

KEY INSIGHT:

Rhetoric Surrounds Us Like a Real-Life Matrix. It Is Often Invisible. It Is Inescapable.

The "No Rhetoric" Style Is a Type of Rhetoric.

The "No Style" Style Is a Style.

SENTIMENT

This one is simple, but powerful. Here it is: Sentiment = pw - nw, where pw = positive words, and nw = negative words. Essentially, this equation determines if the sentiment of your speech is positive or negative. And you can experiment with applying any qualities instead of positive or negative. The problem is that not many dualities are as broad, descriptive, and useful as positive and negative.

Let's break down this equation. If you say 100 words, and 20 of them are positive, and 10 are negative, your sentiment equation yields the number 10: 20 positive words minus 10 negative words. Thus, you have mathematically determined that your communication is positive. But what if you want it to be more positive? This equation is your friend. Add more positive words, or remove the 10 negative words, or replace the 10 negative words with 10 positive words. This equation will instantly help you determine if the overall sentiment if your speech is positive or negative, and it will help you adjust accordingly. With a little effort, this equation can be balanced to adjust for the strength of each individual emotional statement instead of weighing them all equally.

Why is it so important to understand this equation? Clumps of positive words produce certain emotional reactions; clumps of negative words produce certain emotional reactions; and depending on your communication goals, you want one of those reactions. And in some cases, you want a clump of one sentiment, followed by a clump of the other. But what you never want is a sentiment score of 0, unless it is produced by a concentrated, punchy clump of one sentiment followed by its opposite, which numerically cancel out. [pw] [pw] [pw] [pw] [pw] [pw] [nw] [nw] [nw] [nw] [nw] [nw] is effective. Why? Because the two clumps produce two distinct, potent emotional reactions that are strengthened by their contrast, even though the sentiment score is 0, or neutral, over all. This is the limitation of this equation.

Is it really neutral? Is an extreme positive emotional reaction followed by an extreme negative reaction neutral? Mathematically, they cancel out, but in reality, they do not undo each other, they intensify each other, as we will shortly discuss. So, while that example is strong, [pw] [nw] [pw] [nw] [pw] [nw] [pw] [nw] [pw] [nw] [pw] [nw] is not. Why? Because the two opposite sentiments are diffused amongst one another and intertwined in such a way that there is no distinct, unambiguous, unequivocal sentiment prevailing at any point.

What reactions do positive sentiments produce? Elation, elevation, hope, happiness, faith, strength, optimism, and the like.

What reactions do negative sentiments produce? Anger, loss, discomfort, discontent, unhappiness, and the like. So, identify which type of emotional reaction is most likely to bring your audience to the action you want them to take, and use the sentiment equation to gear your words in that direction.

And here's the second rule: If you are speaking for action, avoid a sentiment score of 0 produced by scattered words of opposite sentiment. There will be no compelling emotional reaction. (There might be, depending on whatever else you are doing and saying. However, there will be no compelling emotional reaction as a result of your semantic sentiment).

While a sentiment score of 0 produced by scattered words of opposite sentiment produces no coherent and compelling reaction, a sentiment score of 0 produced by a section with a sentiment score of positive 50 followed by a sentiment score of negative 50 will produce not zero emotional reactions, not one emotional reaction, but two; a positive one, followed by a negative one.

And there is a specific strategy that takes advantage of this mode of sentiment mapping. Contrast a proposed good path (your idea) with an alternative. First, describe the alternative, then describe your proposed path. Use very high negative sentiment when describing the alternative, and very high positive sentiment describing your proposed path. The audience will associate the alternative to your idea with negativity and your idea with positivity. Sure, the sentiment score will be 0 overall, but only because there is first a very high negative sentiment score and then a very high positive sentiment score. And this is not at all neutral. The sentiment score equation is limited by this feature.

We can overcome this limitation if we localize the sentiment score, applying it to specific sections of a communication, instead of the whole. [pw] [pw] [pw] [pw] [pw] [pw] (sentiment score = 6; high positive sentiment score = strong positive emotional reaction) [nw] [nw] [nw] [nw] [nw] [nw] (sentiment score of this section = -6; high negative sentiment score = strong negative emotional reaction).

On the other hand, no matter how you divide up [pw] [nw] [pw] [nw] [pw] [nw] [pw] [nw] [pw] [nw] [pw] [nw] [pw] [nw], you will always have a sentiment score of 0 or near 0, meaning that at any point in your speech, your semantic sentiment is producing no particular emotional reaction (although other things might be). This is a lost opportunity.

Before moving on to our third and final equation, let us examine an example of the sentiment score strategy at play, taken from Donald Trump's 2019 State of the Union address.

"As we have seen, when we are united [+1], we can make astonishing [+1] strides [+1] for our country [+1]. Now, Republicans and Democrats must join [+1] forces again to confront [+1] an urgent [-1] national crisis [-1]. The Congress has 10 days left to pass a bill that will fund [+1] our Government, protect [+1] our homeland [+1], and secure [+1] our southern border. Now is the time for the Congress to show the world that America is committed [+1] to *[dividing line]* ending illegal [-1] immigration and putting the ruthless [-1] coyotes [-1], cartels [-1], drug dealers [-1], and human traffickers [-1] out of business. As we speak, large, organized caravans [-1] are on the march

[-1] to the United States. We have just heard that Mexican cities, in order [-1] to remove the illegal [-1] immigrants from their communities [+1], are getting trucks and buses to bring them up to our country in areas where there is little border protection. I have ordered another 3,750 troops [-1] to our southern border to prepare [+1] for the tremendous [-1] onslaught [-1]."

Note the alternating sentiments: "+ + + + + + - - + + + + + [dividing line] - - - - - - - - - + - + - -"

Observe the overall sentiment rating: 13 positive words minus 14 negative words = -1. This is negligible, and based on the length of the communication, a +3 or -3 range around zero can be regarded as essentially the same as 0.

But remember the limitation of sentiment score, and identify the localized scores on each side of the dividing line (which can be found at the point in communication when a sequence that is extremely positive or negative ends, and is replaced by an opposing sequence). "+ + + + + + - - + + + + +" = 11 positive words minus 2 negative words, with an extremely high positive sentiment score of 9. And across the dividing line, "- - - - - - - - - + - + - -" = 2 positive words minus 12 negative words, with an extremely high negative sentiment score of -10. See the power of localized sentiment? See how applying localization allows us to understand the nuances on a deeper level? And before we get into why Trump used this alternating sentiment strategy, we have to cover one last point: context. Context determines the positive or negative sentiment of certain words. In the first section, "country" is +1. In the second, it is -1.

How can one word have two different sentiment values? Because of where they are, and their context: in the first half, it was a country for which astonishing strides were being accomplished (positive sentiment), and in the second, it was a country in which extreme lengths were taken to deal with what Trump believes is a crisis. This is why, to explore this yet further, we can reengineer the equation to place more emphasis on verbs and adjectives than nouns.

Now, why did Trump do it this way? To produce an extremely strong positive reaction and then an equally strong negative reaction. And the contrast between them makes them more powerful, not less so. Think of it this way: after a sentiment score of +9, the fall to -10 is a fall of -19: 9, 8, 7, 6, 5, 4, 3, 2, 1, 0, -1, -2, -3, -4, -5, -6, -7, -8, -9, -10.

In other words, Trump (or Trump's speechwriters) brought the audience down from a higher point (+9), not from 0, which makes the emotional fall feel more extreme. The impact? The crisis seems more critical; it seems more urgent and more pressing. This is exactly what Trump wanted people to believe.

Further, alternating sentiments are naturally attention-grabbing. Why are they so attention-grabbing? Because the "up and down" pattern of emotional extremes keeps the audience emotionally engaged. Finally – and we discuss this later in its own respect – loss (negative sentiment) hurts more vividly and potently than gain (positive sentiment) satisfies us. So not only did the speechwriters increase the size of the fall, but falls in general are felt more than gains – twice as much, according to some studies. And now, let's move on to our third and final equation.

KEY INSIGHT:

Rhetorical Equations Are Measuring Devices, Designed To Ensure You Are Achieving What You Hope to Achieve.

THE SENTIMENT EQUATION

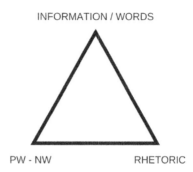

FIGURE 43: Create the desired emotional impact by ensuring that the sentiment equation yields localized extremes.

RHETORIC

Rhetorical power = (logical statements + emotional statements + evidentiary statements) / total number of statements. Rhetorical power is equivalent to the number of statements that use logos, pathos, or ethos divided by the total number of statements. Rhetorical power is the fraction of statements that use one of Aristotle's proven methods of persuasive power. If a statement is both evidence-driven and emotional, that counts as one emotional statement and one evidence-driven statement.

Remember, a statement is not a sentence, but a self-contained, stand-alone thought that can be removed from the communication containing it and retain meaning. In this example, statements are delineated by the <> symbol for clarity.

One final consideration: Weak uses of the rhetorical elements get half-points while strong uses get full points.

This is what Mayor Pete Buttigieg said in one of the 2020 Democratic Primary debates: "We shouldn't have to pay farmers to take the edge off of a trade war <> that shouldn't have been started in the first place <> [+1 logos]. I will support farmers <>, but not long ago, I was in Boone, Iowa <>, a guy came up to me <>, he said I got my Trump bailout check <> [+1 ethos], but I would have rather spent that money on conservation <> [+1 logos]. By the way, this isn't even making farmers whole <> [+1 logos]. If you're in soybeans, for example [+1 ethos], you're getting killed <> [+1 pathos]. And it's not just what this president has done with the trade war <>. In a lot of parts of the country [+0.5 weak ethos], the worst thing is these so-called small refinery waivers <>, which are killing those who are involved in ethanol <> [+1 pathos]. Look, I don't think this president cares one bit about farmers <> [+1 pathos]. He keeps asking them to take one for the team <> [+1 pathos], but more and more I'm talking to people in rural America <> [+1 ethos] who see that they're not going to benefit from business as usual under this president <> [+1 logos]. I believe that so many of the solutions lie with American farmers <>, but we have to stand up for them <> [+0.5 weak pathos], not just with direct subsidies and support, but with making sure we do something about the consolidation <>, the monopolies that leave farmers with fewer places to purchase supplies from and fewer places to sell their product to <> [+1 logos] [+0.5 weak pathos]."

Remember, this is not a perfect science. To make my estimate stronger, I would take 10 (or 100) people with the same experience as me, have them perform this exercise, and then average our scores. But while this isn't exactly 100% precise, it can be very close, and its value is in its comparative use; its value is in how we can compare two speeches, given that the two evaluations are equally imprecise.

This is Pete's score: [(5 logos + 5 pathos + 3.5 ethos) / 20 statements]*100 = 67.5% rhetorical power. Pete Buttigieg is a Rhodes Scholar Harvard Graduate, so I'm sure he is not used to receiving D+ grades. But I implore you to ignore your traditional anchors of good and bad grades when dealing with rhetorical power, and instead apply this method of evaluation: how he stacks up against everyone else on that stage.

I have some recommendations for Mayor Pete. It's nearly impossible to get 100% rhetorical power. And remember, this speech was not prepared, but off-the-cuff. A fully prepared speech is much easier to plan to satisfy this equation. Still, even when speaking in an impromptu manner, this conceptual view of rhetoric will help you become more effective. My recommendations fixate on turning half-points into full-points. As a refresher, these were his half-points: "In a lot of parts of the country... [+0.5 weak ethos]; ...but we have to stand up for them [+0.5 weak pathos]; ...the monopolies that leave farmers with fewer places to purchase supplies from and fewer places to sell their product to [+0.5 weak pathos]"

I challenge you before reading on to think about how you would raise that score. By my experience, here's how full-point rhetorical invocations would have looked in their place: "According to [insert source], in [insert parts] of the country, [insert quantitative claim] [+1 ethos]; ...but we have a moral obligation to support the people who feed our families [+1 pathos]; ...the monopolies that slowly and unfairly choke off American farmers from the American dream and American opportunity [+1 strong pathos]."

Let me be clear: I am not suggesting I would have thought of these phrases in the moment. Hindsight is 20/20, and analyzing a transcript and making recommendations is different from being up on a stage in real-time, speaking from the heart.

We can also split the numerator (the rhetorical devices) into its constituent thirds (each of the devices), and therefore determine how many of the statements are not just rhetorically powerful, but how many use which kind of rhetoric. Then, for example, if you want to give an emotionally driven speech, but find that you have a higher percentage of logos-driven statements than pathos-driven statements, you can adjust accordingly.

THE RHETORIC EQUATION

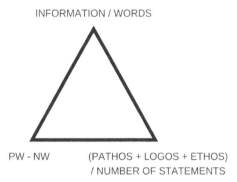

INFORMATION / WORDS

PW - NW　　　(PATHOS + LOGOS + ETHOS)
　　　　　　　/ NUMBER OF STATEMENTS

FIGURE 44: Improve your rhetoric by increasing the proportion of statements that are pathos-driven, logos-driven, and ethos-driven.

THE FOURTH META-EQUATION OF INFLUENCE

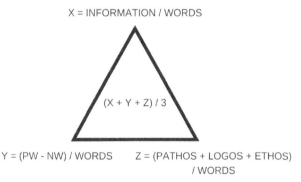

X = INFORMATION / WORDS

(X + Y + Z) / 3

Y = (PW - NW) / WORDS　　Z = (PATHOS + LOGOS + ETHOS)
　　　　　　　　　　　　　　　　/ WORDS

FIGURE 45: A meta-equation emerges out of the three initial equations. Set the substance equation to X, the sentiment equation to Y, and the rhetoric equation to Z. Replace the divisor of each equation with words, adjusting the numerator accordingly. Then add up the proportions of each equation – add up X, Y, and Z – and divide it by three. If the sentiment equation yields a negative, multiply it by negative one before plugging it into the equation. This gives you your average across the three equations. Use it to determine your overall effectiveness.

MICRO-REPETITION

How to directly influence the subconscious mind with a simple model of repetition (that is not obvious and doesn't involve any literal repetition).

The more someone hears a message, the more they believe it. This proven fact of psychology underscores all these strategies. This is the power of positive affirmations: The more you say to yourself, "I'm going to be a phenomenal public speaker," the more you believe it, and the more you believe it, the more likely it comes true.

THE ILLUSORY TRUTH EFFECT VISUALIZED

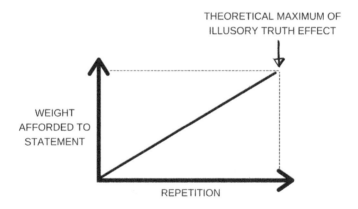

FIGURE 46: As you repeat a message, the weight afforded to the message rises. This is the "the illusory truth effect."

Repetition is a powerful persuasive tool. But it has a caveat. If you want to persuade your audience that your proposed solution is the single solution that can solve their problem, you can't say the following: "This solution is the one solution that can solve your problem. This solution is the one solution that can solve your problem. This solution is the one solution that can solve your problem." Thus, we arrive at the inevitable limitation of the power of repetition. If you apply repetition like this, it will drive people away. In this example, we repeated the message three times in 33 words.

With a clever strategy, we can easily overcome the limitation of repetition, unlocking its persuasive power without sounding crazy. The strategy is micro-repetition. Instead of repeating the core sentiment in literal form three times in 33 words and sounding off-putting, we can say the following: "This unique, specific solution is the one, single, individual key that alone can solve your solution in an unmatched way." This repeats the sentiment that it is the one solution seven times in 20 words, a major improvement. Thus, micro-repetition is the solution to the limitation of persuasive repetition.

KEY INSIGHT:

Repetition Means Retention, and Retention Means Persuasion. What We Repeat Is Up to Us. We Can Repeat the Worst Lies or the Best Moral Truths. Rhetoric Is a Vehicle, not a Destination.

THE SINISTER POWER OF THE ILLUSORY TRUTH EFFECT

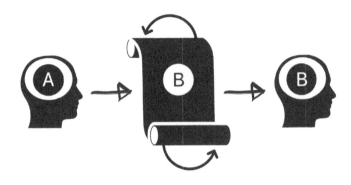

FIGURE 47: Even someone knowing the correct answer changes their response to a questionnaire when repeatedly exposed to the incorrect answer.

Historical Example: "To renew America, we must meet challenges abroad as well at home. There is no longer division between what is foreign and what is domestic; the world economy, the world environment, the world AIDS crisis, the world arms race; they affect us all." – Bill Clinton

THE PEP MODEL

How to instantly apply an easy, step-by-step template to confidently assert your ideas.

Want a proven, simple, step-by-step model that will simplify your communication? If so, the PEP model is for you. It stands for point, evidence, point, and it also uses the power of repetition.

And here's how you can apply a step-by-step process to convert your natural language into this template: Identify the natural statement you want to make. That statement is the first P. Identify the best evidence in favor of this natural statement. That evidence is your E. Identify the best way to restate your original natural statement. That becomes your second P.

Non-PEP (just a P): "We need to expand into developing markets to raise profitability." PEP: "(P) We need to expand into developing markets to raise profitability. (E) For example, India has no competition, and a rising middle-class. (P2) There is massive opportunity in these regions."

See how much more sophisticated, persuasive, compelling and powerful the PEP model is? The second P is the most impactful component: It is more significant than the first because of its repetitive power, but also because the preceding evidence makes it more credible. And the evidence is made more powerful by the first P because it puts it into context. Lacking context, evidence is weak.

You can stretch out the PEP model like an accordion. You can make it PEEEEEP and provide five pieces of evidence if you want.

PEP: "(P) We need to expand into developing markets to raise profitability. (E) For example, India has no competition, and a rising middle-class. (P2) There is massive opportunity in these regions."

PEEEEEBP: "(P) We need to expand into developing markets to raise profitability. (E) For example, India has no competition, and a rising middle-class. (E2) The Boston Consulting group estimates that firms operating there will experience 20% increased stock valuation. (E3) Not to mention the lax regulation in these countries and the strength of the US dollar: we can drastically decrease costs of production, and explosively increase profit margins. (E4) And the talent pool in this country is very high as well: according to the McKinsey group, there are people who are comparatively more educated, but cheaper to employ. (E5) These are some of the many reasons why Warren Buffet shifted significant capital into developing countries and the firms that expand there. (P2) There is massive opportunity in these regions."

I don't necessarily recommend that you stretch it to five pieces of evidence. You be the judge of that, based on your situation. I just want to let you know that you can. It depends on the paradigm of the situation, which only you can determine. Is it primarily two-way communication, or one-way communication? Where does it lie on that spectrum? If lies toward two-way communication, five pieces of evidence might seem like a monologue, which often doesn't work in that paradigm. However, if it lies toward one-way communication, five pieces of evidence are appropriate. If it is a two-way situation where a small number of people are not competing for speaking time, go for the lengthy PEEEEP. If there are 30 people who want to speak in a meeting that is 30 minutes long, go with PEP, unless you don't mind getting a disproportionate share of the time.

And keep in mind the concept of diminishing returns: Every additional piece of evidence compels and persuades, but not as much as the one before it. Often, evidence is just a check-box that people must quickly check in their minds before they will allow their emotion to take over their logic.

Finally, if you stretch out to over three portions of evidence, you must include a bridge (B), that enumerates the significance of the evidence: PEEEEEBP: "(P) We need to expand into developing markets to raise profitability. (E) For example, India has no competition, and a rising middle-class. (E2) The Boston Consulting group estimates that firms operating there will experience 20% increased stock valuation. (E3) Not to mention the lax regulation in these countries and the strength of the US dollar: we can drastically decrease costs of production, and explosively increase profit margins. (E4) And the talent pool in this country is very high as well: according to the McKinsey group, there are people who are comparatively more educated, but cheaper to employ. (E5) These are some of the many reasons why Warren Buffet shifted significant capital into developing countries and the firms that expand there. (B) All this credible evidence unequivocally proves that (P2) there is massive opportunity in these regions."

The bridge connects your evidence back to your point, because after five pieces of evidence, you need to refresh the relationship. And the bridge is assertive. You have provided five pieces of evidence, so you have earned the right to say your position has been unequivocally proven by credible evidence.

With multiple points, you can produce the following structure: PEP, PEP, PEP.

THE P QUANT QUAL P MODEL

How to use a proven strategy that guarantees persuasion, power and influence.

There are two types of evidence, and you need them both for maximum persuasion. As a refresher, here they are: quantitative evidence and qualitative evidence. You can regard the first kind as primarily logical, and the second as primarily emotional. Numerical evidence is quantitative. Stories, examples, and anecdotes are qualitative. Quantitative evidence appeals to the logical mind and builds certainty. The subsequent qualitative evidence appeals to the emotional mind, where influence actually occurs.

You need quantitative evidence. It brings down the guard of the logical, disconfirming mind. Then you can punch straight at the emotional mind with an emotional qualitative example. If you go straight to the qualitative, you leave behind logical persuasion. You leave people hot but unconvinced. If you skip the qualitative and only use quantitative, you leave people convinced but cold. People are naturally horrible at dealing with statistics and much better at dealing with anecdotes and stories. But for the anecdotes and stories to take effect, you need to earn logical permission by presenting a strong quantitative case for your position. So, an adaptation of the PEP (point, evidence, point) model is the P Quant Qual P model. And you can stretch it out: P Quant Qual Quant Qual Quant Qual P model.

THE PSYCHOLOGY OF THE P, QUANT, QUAL, P STRUCTURE

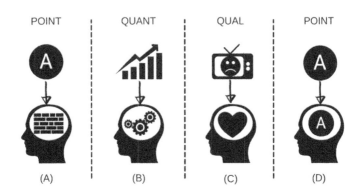

FIGURE 48: Flatly stating the point tends to bounce off of the cognitive defenses of the audience members with more frequency than a more sophisticated approach (A). Flatly stating the point is the beginning of this approach, whereas most speakers treat it as both the beginning and the end. The next step is revealing the quantitative evidence, which appeals to the logical, evidence-driven mind (B). Using a qualitative example next appeals to the emotional mind (C). It is ethos and logos (B) followed by pathos (C). The repetition of the point drives it home (D). (B) and (C) break down the cognitive defenses (A) and communicate the point effectively (D). Keep in mind that the repetition of the point need not be strict repetition. Restate the point in different words. After the quantitative and qualitative steps, you have the leeway to state the point in a more forceful, rhetorically charged form.

Point: "We need to solve income inequality." Quantitative evidence: "The top 1% made 50% of all new income in the past year." Qualitative evidence: "I spoke with a family in Iowa's fourth district; the father hasn't seen his kids in a week, since he works a night shift at his third job when they go to bed, and the mother had to drop out of school and give up her dreams to make ends, barely, just barely, meet." Point Repetition: "It's time to fix this now."

Historical Example: "I think we're for aiding our allies by sharing of our material blessings with those nations which share in our fundamental beliefs, but we're against doling out money government to government, creating bureaucracy, if not socialism, all over the world. We set out to help 19 countries. We're helping 107. We've spent 146 billion dollars. With that money, we bought a 2-million-dollar yacht for Haile Selassie. We bought dress suits for Greek undertakers, extra wives for Kenyan government officials. We bought a thousand TV sets for a place where they have no electricity. In the last six years, 52 nations have bought 7 billion dollars' worth of our gold, and all 52 are receiving foreign aid from this country." – Ronald Reagan

LOSS VERSUS GAINS

How to instantly grab audience attention and motivate enthusiastic action.

People feel and fear losses more than they feel and hope for gains. A loss of $1,000 hurts people more than they a gain of $1,000 pleases them. In fact, some people, in some situations, feel losses twice as strongly as they feel gains.

So, in light of the fact that emotional impact is what produces action, how do you think you can use the information I just gave you? You can center your audience benefits not only on some gain, but on the prevention of some loss. This will make your proposal a much more compelling offer. Of course, the best case is to do both, and center the benefit on some gain and the prevention of some loss.

Loss aversion is the name of this phenomenon, and loss aversion pushes us to take mathematically illogical choices to reduce a very infinitesimally small chance of loss to zero. So, you can engineer that into your communication too. You can use the fact that people overweigh tiny reductions in risk if the risk is reduced to zero. The reduction in risk from 2% to 0% is significantly more attractive than a reduction in risk from 12% to 10%, even though the reductions are mathematically equivalent. And the reduction in risk from 2% to 0% can be weighed even more favorably than the reduction in risk from 10% to 2%, for example. Loss aversion pushes people to hate any risk, even a tiny one. Use this to your advantage by emphasizing certainty of outcome, if you have it.

Instead of framing the offer as "do X, and you will gain Y," say this: "do X, and you will gain Y while preventing the loss of Z."

WHERE DOES EMOTIONAL IMPACT COME FROM?

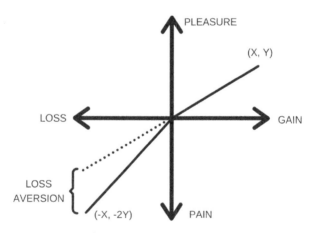

FIGURE 49: Loss often produces up to two times as much pain as an equivalent gain does pleasure.

Historical Example: "As for the peace that we would preserve, I wonder who among us would like to approach the wife or mother whose husband or son has died in South Vietnam and ask them if they think this is a peace that should be maintained indefinitely. Do they mean peace, or do they mean we just want to be left in peace?

There can be no real peace while one American is dying some place in the world for the rest of us. *We're at war with the most dangerous enemy that has ever faced mankind in his long climb from the swamp to the stars, and it's been said if we lose that war, and in so doing lose this way of freedom of ours, history will record with the greatest astonishment that those who had the most to lose did the least to prevent its happening.* Well I think it's time we ask ourselves if we still know the freedoms that were intended for us by the Founding Fathers." – Ronald Reagan

---

KEY INSIGHT:

As Long as We Exist, We Exist at a Crossroad: An Eternal Juncture, An Inescapable Fork In the Road, With One Path Leading Down, One Path Leading Up, And All Manner of Temptations Beckoning Us Downward.

Fearing the Downward Path Is the Price of Not Following It.

THE SELF-CHESS STRATEGY

How to quickly understand the "first principles" of your argument.

If you do this before every debate or verbal altercation, you will gain crystal-clarity on the fundamental first principles of your position. This strategy will help you identify the core logical principles and value judgements at the heart of your argument, pushing through the muck of externalities and irrelevancies, and extracting the elegant truths that will win people over.

Step one: Reduce your argument to one thesis, like "X should Y," for example. Step two: Put yourself in the shoes of your opponent (like you are playing chess against yourself and you just flipped around the board), and with honest effort, try to counterargue against your own thesis. Step three: Flip the board back around, and counterargue against the previously counterarguments. Step four: Repeat until you arrive at an inalienable logical truth and core principle of your argument; repeat until you arrive at something irrefutable. Step five: Repeat for all possible rebuttals in step two, chasing every logical thread down to its end. Step six: Write down the core logical principles you found at the end of the threads, but track the threads themselves, because your opponents might jump in with a counterargument that exists at any point on the thread between thesis to core logical principle. The more thoroughly and honestly you do this, the greater the chance that you will predict the exact pattern of an argument, giving yourself an opportunity to prepare.

KEY INSIGHT:

Crusade Against Your Cherished Beliefs. Cherish the Survivors More.

DISCOVERING THE FIRST PRINCIPLES OF YOUR POSITION

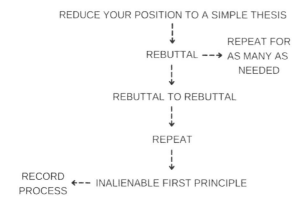

FIGURE 50: This process helps you elucidate the first principles of your position. It reveals the core of your stance, and speaking in terms of these deeply impactful first principles grants you immense influence.

In its very nature, this strategy mirrors the course of an honest intellectual debate. Person one advances an argument. Person two counters it. Person one counters the counter. Person two counters the counter to their counter. They continue until one of them arrives at an inalienable logical truth with which the other cannot argue. At every stage of the argument, what they were really doing was stripping away externalities to try to reach the logical core together.

But what if you could skip the whole debacle, and start at the core? What if you can avoid having to risk missing it altogether by getting lost in the weeds of a debate that doesn't gradually move toward the core logical truths of the matter at hand? That's exactly what this strategy will do for you, provided you do it correctly, which above all means really putting yourself in the shoes of your opponent and trying to debunk your stance. You will be able to start with the inalienable logical truths, and argue with clarity and confidence.

And if you do this thoroughly, you will not only argue with clarity and confidence, but you will also anticipate every possible argument of your opponent and have a prepared response.

THE GROUP-CHESS STRATEGY

How to gain crystal clarity, complete confidence, and 100% accuracy in your ideas.

This is a powerful strategy. Prior to the vast majority of my successes as a nationally recognized competitive public speaker, I did this with some trusted confidants, and I would not have succeeded the way I did if it weren't for this strategy.

The main challenge of the self-chess strategy is being effective at arguing against your own position. With this strategy, you don't have to. Get your friends involved (people who won't be in the actual discussion), and ask them to argue against your positions. And I promise you this: If you apply this method, you will predict and preempt the vast majority of arguments your opponents will advance. It will be much easier to garner insight into your opposition's stances if you let other people play that role. Find friends who are sharp, verbally skilled, honest, and willing to play the part of your opponent comfortably, as well as friends who truly believe the perspective of your opponents and have done their research. It is the same as runners training in thin-air environments like the Colorado mountains: When they return to a normal environment, they are seriously empowered. Train with the hardest possible opponent: Do everything you can do to ensure that your "sparring partner" is better than your real opponent.

MAXIMIZING THE EFFECTIVENESS OF THIS APPROACH

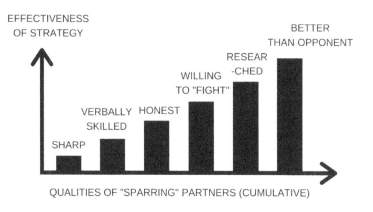

FIGURE 51: As the qualities rise, so does the efficacy of this strategy, Note that the bars are cumulative.

And the benefits extend yet further: These people can give you a wide range of feedback. A little too derisive on a rebuttal? A little slow to concede some obviously incorrect points? A little too abrasive, or a little too soft? These people, if they are invested in your success, will help you identify these errors.

GROUP PRACTICE

How to guarantee your communication will be suave, eloquent, and polished.

If I worked in sales, the first thing I would do is gather together a group of my coworkers and practice our pitches and objection-handling together for 30 minutes a day. One person delivers, the other people give feedback (perhaps written on paper for permanence), then another goes, so on and so forth, until everyone has gone and received feedback. Then run another round incorporating the first-round feedback. And again, after that, and again and again and again until every single person speaks with perfect eloquence, convincing confidence, extremely effective vocal modulation and delivery, and excellent body language.

And after everyone has their memorized pitches perfected, what then? Apply the group practice principle to what comes after the pitch, whatever that may be. Objection-handling? Question and answer segments? Whatever it is, run through it as a group, and make it rigorous and challenging.

THE GROUP-BASED IMPROVEMENT CYCLE

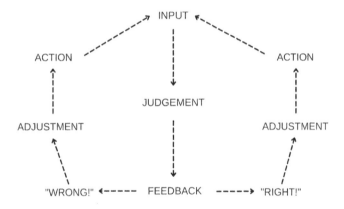

FIGURE 52: You provide a communication input to your group. They judge it. They provide this feedback to you. Either they judge it to be "right" or "wrong." You adjust as needed, and this produces a modified action. This modified action serves as another input, repeating the cycle.

You will all experience incredible improvement. Whatever the upcoming communication situation is, if the stakes are high enough, use this strategy.

THE OBJECTION PREDICTION MODEL

How to predict exactly why your audience might disagree and diffuse their objections.

What is it? Predicting the reasons your audience might object to your offer, then structuring your speech around addressing them.

Why does it work? It removes all the reasons your audience wouldn't accept your call to action. It clears the most common barriers to action. It leaves your audience no logical reason to not act.

When do you use it? When you have to persuade an audience. When you have to make a sales pitch. When you predict opposition.

What is the step-by-step process? Discovery phase: Discover the most common, probable objections to your proposal. Invalidation phase: Invalidate the objections. Construction phase: Construct your speech around the reasons why those objections are invalid. Presentation phase: Present a speech constructed around invalidating the objections you've discovered.

THE OBJECTION-PREDICTION MODEL VISUALIZED

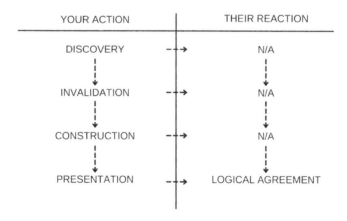

FIGURE 53: The objection-prediction model is highly effective at convincing the audience logically. Further emotional persuasion may be required.

This one removes all the reasons your audience won't do what you want. When you are persuading someone, you will be met with persuasion resistance. Persuasion resistance often takes the form of specific objections to your offer, idea, or proposal. Here are some common examples: "I don't want to give anything up for it (which is a form of loss aversion: spending feels like a loss). I don't believe it can work. I don't think it can work for me. I can wait. I think it's too difficult. I don't understand it. I don't understand why I need it. I don't believe it will do what is promised. I don't know if it fits into my life. I don't trust the speaker." This structure dissolves concerns.

Counter each objection at the exact moment you think your audience might be thinking it. Counter the right objections: Don't counter objections that people don't have. If you are a trustworthy authority, then trusting you isn't a common objection. In this case, don't talk about your credentials over and over. You would be countering an objection that doesn't exist. Do not directly state the objections. Only say your counters. Don't say, "Now you might be thinking it costs too much, but it's $3,000 less than our competitors." Instead, just say "It's $3,000 less than our competitors." Stating the objection puts it in their heads if they weren't thinking about it.

KEY INSIGHT:

Line Up All the Reasons You Might Be Wrong, Honestly Consider Them One at a Time, And Accept the Outcome.

HOW TO OVERCOME ANY OBJECTION IN 10 SECONDS

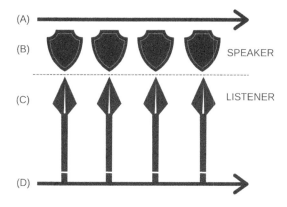

FIGURE 54: The internal monologue of your listener (D) runs parallel to and reacts to your message (A). As you make claims (perhaps about how something works), the internal monologue throws out objections to your claims (C) (perhaps about how it won't work for them). These objections may or may not be voiced out loud. However, "even if" statements preempt or overcome these objections by stating that your main claim remains true in spite of the thing they thought would debunk your claim. Thus, they act as shields (B) that protect your claim (A) from the objections (C) thrown out in your audience's internal monologue (D). This relies on predicting the probable objections at play (and at which point they are most likely to arise).

This structure is four steps that remove all barriers your audience has to accepting your offer (assuming you do it right).

Historical Example: "Socialism is a scare word they have hurled at every advance the people have made in the last 20 years. *Socialism is what they called public power. Socialism is what they called social security. Socialism is what they called farm price supports. Socialism is what they called bank deposit insurance. Socialism is what they called the growth of free and independent labor organizations. Socialism is their name for almost anything that helps all the* *people.* When the Republican candidate inscribes the slogan 'Down With Socialism' on the banner of his 'great crusade,' that is really not what he means at all. What he really means is 'Down with Progress – down with Franklin Roosevelt's New Deal,' and 'down with Harry Truman's fair Deal.' That's all he means." – Harry Truman

---

KEY INSIGHT:

Understanding Rhetorical Devices Offers You Two Powerful Abilities:

To Use Them for Good And To Resist Those Who Choose To Use Them Differently.

"LET'S" STATEMENTS

How to motivate anyone to do anything with one simple word.

An absurd amount of the world's most moving inspirational speeches by world-leaders and earth-shakers ubiquitously use one simple phrase over and over again: "let us."

Are you the leader of a team? If so, this is for you. Want to describe to your audience members – your subordinates – what you want them to do, in a way that is authoritative and assertive but not bossy and annoying? If so, this is for you.

Instead of saying, for example, "go to the national sales conference and get as many contacts as possible," say "let's go to the national sales conference and get as many contacts as possible."

Why? Because adding one simple word completely shifts the tone of the message. It is not an individual, despotic order anymore. Instead, it is a team directive. It is "let us," not "I, your boss, want you to do this, or else." It emphasizes the team and builds unity. And it takes off the pressure without blurring the clarity of your directives.

It makes it seem like a team effort. And if the responsibility will belong to one specific person, follow the "let's statement" with a question like this: "[insert name], do you think you can take care of that for us?"

This is a sort of micro-reframing, because it changes the situation from "I want you to do this for me," to "let's do this for us."

Historical Example: "What General Weygand called the Battle of France is over. I expect that the Battle of Britain is about to begin. Upon this battle depends the survival of Christian civilization. Upon it depends our own British life, and the long continuity of our institutions and our Empire. The whole fury and might of the enemy must very soon be turned on us. Hitler knows that he will have to break us in this Island or lose the war. If we can stand up to him, all Europe may be free and the life of the world may move forward into broad, sunlit uplands. But if we fail, then the whole world, including the United States, including all that we have known and cared for, will sink into the abyss of a new Dark Age made more sinister, and perhaps more protracted, by the lights of perverted science. *Let us* therefore brace ourselves to our duties, and so bear ourselves that, if the British Empire and its Commonwealth last for a thousand years, men will still say, 'This was their finest hour.'" – Winston Churchill

THE "WHY DON'T YOU" PHRASE

How to use a simple phrase to instantly get people to do what you want without pressure.

Just like "let's" phrases reframe "I want you to do this for me" to "let's do this for us," the "why don't you" phrase subtly reframes a situation to your advantage.

Instead of saying "do X" which implies the question "why should I?" say "why don't you do X?" which changes the frame from "I need to be given reasons to do X" to "I need to give reasons to not do X." This is a much more disarming frame, and it is much less likely to receive resistance.

VISUALIZING THE SUBTLE MICRO-REFRAMING

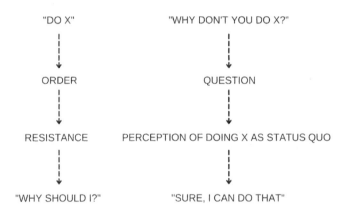

FIGURE 55: People have a tendency to resist direct commands and orders. This strategy circumvents their resistance, yielding more positive results.

THE RIVER OF YOU

How to achieve captivating and engaging communication.

This one secret of effective communication will completely change the way you see successful speaking. One of the most captivating, engaging, and attention-grabbing ways to allow your words words go directly to the minds of your audience members in the exact form that your intuition served them up to you. One of the most effective forms of communication is a direct, unfiltered, unfettered river of your consciousness into your audience's consciousness.

So how does this change the way you see effective communication? All you have to do to be a captivating, eloquent, and perfect communicator is to remove the inhibitions from the path of this river of your consciousness and let it flow effortlessly and naturally, directly into the minds of your audience members.

This is the hardest thing to achieve fully. But you don't have to remove every inhibition to see the impact; every single obstacle you remove brings you a little closer to this ideal state, and therefore every single obstacle you can remove is worth removing, even if you know you can't remove them all.

I know I have never removed them all. But I have gotten close. And the result was the most incredible thing I have ever experienced. There was nearly nothing in between me and my audience. The words came out, and they came out beautifully, with technically excellent delivery, all because I just let them go – I let it all go – and spoke with total presence in the moment, with almost zero negative inhibitions.

KEY INSIGHT:

To Succeed In the Moment That Matters, Forget Everything But the Moment.

EFFORTLESSLY CHANNELING A SUPERIOR INTELLIGENCE

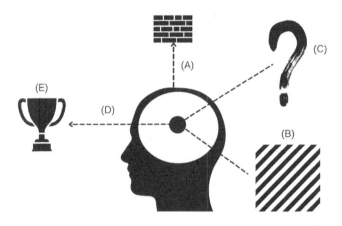

FIGURE 56: Lifting your inhibitions and unblocking your latent power (A) allows the immense intelligence of your subconscious mind (B) and other forms of intellgence (C) to channel through you, producing perfect performance (D) that achieves your goal (E).

THE SECRET OF WHY I KEPT FAILING

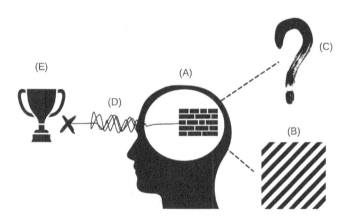

FIGURE 57: Whenever I performed poorly as a communicator, it was because I blocked the flow (A) of my subconscious (B) and – I believe, but you may believe otherwise, and that's okay – a higher power (C). As a

result, I produced poor outputs (D) that fell short of my goals (E).

UNDERSTANDING WHERE OUR INHIBITIONS COME FROM

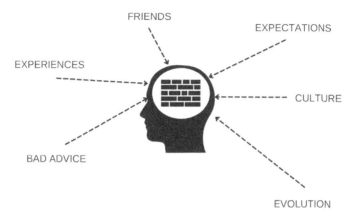

FIGURE 58: Many experiences instill inhibitions, but only our acceptance matters. We have the first and only say. We can refuse to accept any would-be inhibition.

RECOGNIZING HIDDEN, SELF-DEFEATING INHIBITIONS

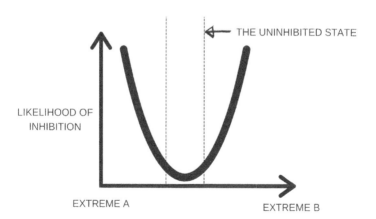

FIGURE 59: Extremes are more likely to be inhibiting thought patterns than balanced qualities, which tend to be both virtues and accurate beliefs about the world. Confidence, for example, is both a belief and a quality, and

it is balanced and accurate. Arrogance is one extreme and insecurity is another.

A common obstacle is anxiety. Why is public speaking and communication anxiety harmful to your communication? Because it is an obstacle on the path of this river of you.

OPEN RAPPORT

How to draw people in with one simple secret of vocal tonality and modulation.

Try not to use open rapport except in your personal introduction. Open rapport, or question tonality, is how you speak when you indicate a question; the pitch goes up at the end of the sentence. And when you are making authoritative statements, you should never apply this tonality, because it makes you seem unsure about your statements, undermining your credibility.

If this is true, why should you use them in your personal introduction? Because this fatal flaw of open rapport tonality (namely that it makes your statements seem like questions and therefore makes you seem uncertain) does not apply to statements which you are obviously certain about, like your personal introduction. And if you can think of other statements for which your certainty is unquestionable, then use open rapport for those too.

Why use open rapport for these specific kinds of statements? Because, as the name suggests, we are psychologically programmed to hear open rapport tonality as the opening of a rapport; as the start of a two-way interaction that demands our attention.

When someone asks you a question, which is in some cases only indicated by this open rapport tonality, you know you must allocate them some of your attention. Open rapport tonality subconsciously signals to people that they need to give the speaker attention.

BREAKING RAPPORT

How to immediately portray immense confidence and value with another secret of vocal tonality.

Breaking rapport, the opposite of open rapport, is the vocal tonality in which your pitch goes down at the end of your sentence. It makes you seem confident, offers your statements sound more certain and assertive, and garners you an air of conclusion. It signals the authoritative, confident, clear-cut end of a unit of meaning.

I have witnessed this in televised political debates time and time again: When a speaker ends his turn without using breaking-rapport, it sounds extremely awkward. It sounds snipped. It sounds like he just got cut-off, not like he intentionally came to a forceful, rhetorically- and verbally-well-punctuated end. People are not sure if he really finished.

And it's a spectrum: When you are speaking, the sharper the breaking rapport tonality, the greater the sense of conclusion. If you are ending a unit of meaning in your communication and don't use breaking rapport, there is a weak signal of conclusion and it sounds like your sentence was snipped in half and the actual conclusion of the sentence was left out. Use breaking rapport for most statements of your core content, and use even sharper breaking rapport for your concluding or essential statements. The sharper the breaking-rapport (the further pitch goes down), the more conclusive a statement sounds.

KEY INSIGHT:

Subtle Vocal Strategies Can Make the Difference Between a Message Sinking or Swimming.

THE THREE VOCAL TONALITIES

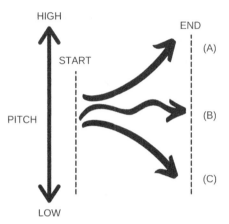

FIGURE 60: Open rapport tonality ends your sentence at a higher pitch than its starting pitch (A). Even tonality ends your sentence at roughly the same pitch as its starting pitch (B). Breaking rapport tonality ends your sentence at a lower pitch than its starting pitch (C).

THE GREATER THE BREAK, THE GREATER THE PUNCH

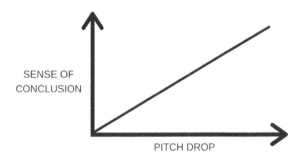

FIGURE 61: The greater the extent of the breaking rapport, the stronger the sense of conclusion.

An advanced strategy is to use the rhetorical technique of hypophora (a rhetorical question followed by its answer – "Why does this happen? Because…"), delivering the question portion with open rapport and the answer portion with breaking rapport. This makes your answer seem especially certain. It also provides variance, creates contrast between tonalities, and creates a two-fold benefit: attention opt-in from the open rapport, and the appearance of confident certainty from the breaking rapport.

KEY INSIGHT:

Our Nervous Systems Take in an Incalculable Number of Inputs, Consciously and Unconsciously.

Judgment is the Result of Reason Acting on These Inputs, As Well As Past (And Anticipated) Inputs.

Email Peter D. Andrei, the author of the Speak for Success collection and the President of Speak Truth Well LLC directly.

pandreibusiness@gmail.com

THE THEORY OF DEGREES OF INTENSITY

How to immediately raise the stakes and grab attention.

For every meaningful word in a sentence, there are a set of synonyms that deliver the same meaning with more intensity and a set that does so with less intensity. You can interchange them to suit your needs. In addition to interchanging words in this manner, you can tag attached adjectives onto a sentence that lessen or heighten intensity and enumerations that intensify or relax as well.

In a broader sense, every sentence exists in a hierarchy of intensity with every other possible way of saying the same thing, and this hierarchy is arranged by ascending intensity.

HOW TO STOKE A MOTIVATIONAL INFERNO

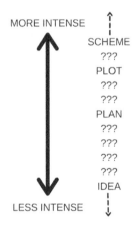

FIGURE 62: You can turn any statement into a more or less intense version of itself. There are potentially infinite positions on the spectrum.

Consider this sentence from the first presidential debate of 2016, spoken by Hillary Clinton: "and the kind of plan that Donald has put forth would be trickle-down economics all over again."

First, identify the words that the "interchange" principle of this theory can best act upon: "and the kind of <u>plan</u> that Donald has put forth would be trickle-down economics all over again."

Then, interchange the words with their less or (in this case) more intense counterparts: "and the kind of *scheme* that Donald has put forth would be trickle-down economics all over again."

Then, identify all nouns to which you can attach an adjective: "and this <u>kind</u> of *<u>scheme</u>* that Donald has put forth would be <u>trickle-down economics</u> all over again."

Then, attach the intensifying adjectives: "and this *short-sighted* kind of *simplistic* scheme that Donald has put forth would be *failed* trickle-down economics all over again."

Now, this example only showed you the interchanging of words to achieve higher degrees of intensity and the tagging on of attached adjectives to raise intensity. So, what about the broad theory? Let me show you how we can completely rework this sentence to become one of its friends near the top of the intensity hierarchy.

What she said: "And the kind of plan that Donald has put forth would be trickle-down economics all over again." What the two-part basic tenets of the theory made it: "and this short-sighted kind of simplistic scheme that Donald has put forth would be failed trickle-down economics all over again." What she could have said (in other words, a sentence near the top of the intensity hierarchy with the same meaning): "And the dangerous, ineffective, broken scheme Donald presented would once more shackle us to the failed ideology of trickle-down economics, and the death of the middle class, rebirth of recession, and economic self-destruction that comes with it."

The reason I provide the two tenets first is that they function in an algorithmic way: in a step-by-step manner, they modify the sentence as needed. Why is this valuable? Because the jump from the initial sentence to the one I designed is much less obvious, and for people who have not yet developed this type of intuition, the algorithmic model is more accessible.

That said, is the sentence with higher intensity better? That is not for me to decide. All I can say is that it is more intense. I provide the tools. It is up to you to use them however you see fit.

Although the subtext and simplification of the sentence is "Donald Trump wants to advance a bad plan." The first sentence (what she actually said) delivered that subtext and simplified message. In this case, delivering that message with more intensity would seem to be to her advantage.

HOW TO EASE THE PRESSURE, HOW TO RAISE IT

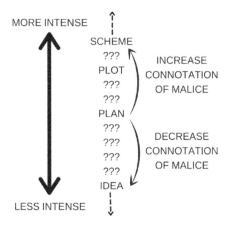

FIGURE 63: Intensity in a broader sense refers to the strength of the qualities the item displays. Terror is more intense than fear; to shred is more intense than to rip; a scheme connotes more malice than an idea.

Historical Example: "You and I have a *rendezvous* with *destiny.* We'll preserve *for our children* this, the *last best hope* of man *on Earth,* or we'll *sentence* them to take the *last step* into a *thousand years* of *darkness.*" – Ronald Reagan

AUDIENCE CHARACTERISTIC MODEL

How to quickly ensure that your audience cares about your words instead of tuning out.

I might be called reductionist for all these algorithmic models, but they can be incredibly powerful, and not at all forced. Why? Because they become part of you. I don't think about these algorithmic step-by-step strategies anymore. They are a part of me. They happen subconsciously, in a fraction of a second, like all skills will with practice.

This is another algorithm: Identify your message. Identify your audience persona. Reengineer your message to speak to that audience persona.

THE RIGHT MESSAGE TO THE WRONG AUDIENCE

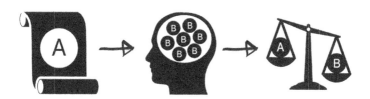

FIGURE 64: If your audience has a strong set of opposing preexisting beliefs, your message may fall flat simply because their preconditioning outweighs it.

Before we get into the why, let's take care of the what. What is an audience persona? Your audience's needs. Your audience's beliefs. Your audience's values. Your audience's objections. Your audience's pain points. Your audience's preconceptions about you. Your audience's value hierarchy. Your audience's past experiences with speakers like you. Your audience's past experiences with ideas like yours. Your audience's past experience with similar situations. Your audience's driving desires.

Identify these with particular emphasis on what all of your audience is likely to share and then make sure your message caters directly to this vivid persona. This will guarantee you don't alienate yourself from your audience or break the fragile speaker-to-audience connection, and that you have a better understanding of what makes them tick. It also gives you a better chance of getting undivided attention and earning their respect.

Remember the river of you? Remember the uninhibited stream of your consciousness into your audience's consciousness? One major inhibition is streaming your consciousness into the wrong recipient – one who only exists in your mind, not in the real world. Your consciousness flows differently when you remove the inhibition of a wrong or incomplete idea of who your audience members are.

WHAT HAPPENS IF YOU DON'T KNOW YOUR AUDINECE?

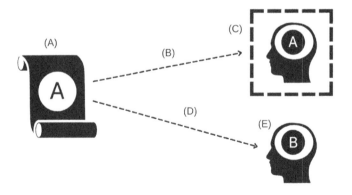

FIGURE 65: When you form a message designed to mesh with people who believe a certain proposition (A) and begin to stream this consciousness, be careful that you are not

streaming it (B) to an imaginary audience. Ensure that you are not misreading the audience and streaming this message (D) to an audience for which it is not designed (E). Give the right message to the right audience.

But what if your message has absolutely nothing to do with your audience persona? What if there is a poor message-to-audience match? Apply alignment. We can update our algorithm to include this: Identify your message. Identify your audience persona. Is your message a good fit to your audience persona? If yes, stop here. Is your message a decent fit to your audience persona, but could be better with some tweaking? If yes, reengineer your message to speak to that audience persona, and stop here. Is your message a poor fit to your audience persona? Do you need some major work to make it fit the persona? If yes, use alignment

ALIGNMENT OFFERS YOU IMPACT AND INFLUENCE

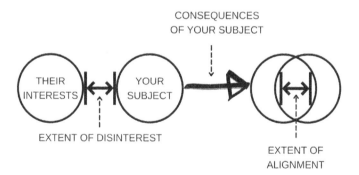

FIGURE 66: The extent of their disinterest is equal to the extent of the gap between what you're talking about and what they care about. By introducing a more compelling consequence of your subject, you can align the two.

And what is alignment? In simple terms, it is connecting the poorly-fitting subject to a well-fitting subject. It is taking your message, connecting it to something your audience cares about, and speaking in a synthesis of these two things. It is speaking in terms of the connections between your intended subject and your audience's interests if the two are not one and the same.

THE HALO EFFECT

How to use a proven psychological principle to make everything you say sound better.

Many of these strategies work because of the fundamental quirks and functions of human psychology. And the halo effect is a perfect example of that. If people initially perceive one good quality in you (or in anything), that one good quality generates a "halo" of unobserved positive qualities: The confident person becomes confident, smart, attentive, and capable. The research on this is conclusive. Portray one good quality early, and that good quality will spill over and define the way people see you more broadly. Portray one bad quality early and the same will happen. It will spill over into how people define you overall.

What is the moral of this as it relates to communication? Portray one good quality in an undeniable and distinct but graceful and classy manner early on. This will kick up the halo effect and that one good quality will make people perceive you as good overall. If they perceive you as good overall, they will be more likely to perceive your message as good overall.

Why does it matter what they think of you? Shouldn't only your message matter? The halo effect certainly applies to your message too, but the truth is this: People substitute the hard question of "what do I think of this message?" with the easy question of "what do I think of the message's source?"

Try this experiment: Go to a group of Democrats who supported Hillary Clinton, give them Donald Trump's inaugural address, tell them it was her planned inaugural address, and see what they think of it. They will substitute "what do I think of this message?" with "what do I think of this message's source?" They will do this without realizing it, and they will not dislike the address as much as they would have if they knew its true source.

The *ad hominem* – or "against the person" – logical fallacy is the most common of them all. To achieve logical clarity, people should separate a message from its source and evaluate it on its own merit, but they don't. Cater to the common fallacy, not by making an opponent's character seem bad, but by making your character seem good, so that your message appears good when your audience reneges on the question of "is the message good?" and opts for the easy question: "do I like its source?"

KEY INSIGHT:

The Greatest Belief Someone Can Have About a Leader Is That "They Will Tell Me the Truth."

Trust Takes Time to Earn. Once Earned, Everything Is Easier. But It Takes Seconds to Lose.

MASTER THE PSYCHOLOGY OF FIRST IMPRESSIONS

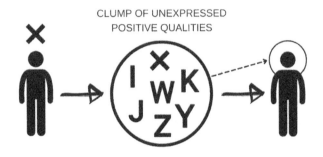

FIGURE 67: When people perceive positive quality "X" in you, the halo effect causes them to also judge you as possessing a clump of unexpressed positive qualities.

So, to summarize, use the halo effect early on for both yourself and your message. How? By quickly portraying one good quality of yourself and of your message in a distinct way. Don't force it. If you come right out and say "I'm [insert good quality]," what you'll actually portray will be "I'm full of myself." Subtlety is key. Just because something is clear and deliberate doesn't mean it can't be achieved with suave subtlety.

Historical Example: "President Pitzer, Mr. Vice President, Governor, Congressman Thomas, Senator Wiley, and Congressman Miller, Mr. Webb, Mr. Bell, scientists, distinguished guests, and ladies and gentlemen: I appreciate your president having made me an honorary visiting professor, and I will assure you that my first lecture will be very brief. I am delighted to be here, and I'm particularly delighted to be here on this occasion. We meet at a college noted for knowledge, in a city noted for progress, in a State noted for strength, and we stand in need of all three, for we meet in an hour of change and challenge, in a decade of hope and fear, in an age of both knowledge and ignorance. The greater our knowledge increases, the greater our ignorance unfolds." – John F. Kennedy

EXCLUSIVITY PHRASES

How to trigger people's subconscious driver toward the scarce in your favor.

Many core psychological human drives push us toward the exclusive, the in-demand, and the scarce. So, how do you use this in your communication? By applying exclusivity phrases. Sprinkle words like "exclusive," "rare," and "hard to come by" around your proposal. These simple words have a complicated impact. They subtly and subconsciously invoke the many core human drives and desires that push people toward exclusivity.

A PROVEN PROCESS FOR MOTIVATING DESIRE

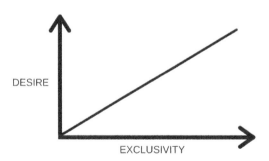

FIGURE 68: When the exclusivity of something rises, so does the extent to which people desire it. More accurately, this relationship deals with perceived exclusivity. If actual exclusivity rises while perceived exclusivity drops, then desire drops. In France, to persuade the public to eat potatoes (which were perceived as "lowly" by the population), the government guarded the potato fields. Perceived exclusivity and scarcity rose, and so did desire.

People began eating potatoes. However, true exclusivity and scarcity dropped – they were (probably) more plentiful than ever.

No exclusivity phrases: "This portfolio beats the market by 5% on average, and usually yields 3% in biannual dividend payments."

Many exclusivity phrases: "This *exclusive, limited-access* portfolio outperforms the market by an *extremely rare* 5% average, and also yields a 3% *bonus* payment in biannual dividends."

I used four exclusivity phrases. You can use many more. But there are different types of exclusivity: exclusivity of information, exclusivity of access, and exclusivity of priority are some of the most effective. The previous example used access.

One kind of exclusivity phrase: "This *exclusive, limited-access* portfolio outperforms the market by an *extremely rare* 5% average, and also yields a 3% *bonus* payment in biannual dividends."

Three kinds of exclusivity phrases: "[Exclusivity of access] This *exclusive, limited-access* portfolio outperforms the market by an *extremely rare* 5% average, and also yields a 3% *bonus* payment in biannual dividends. [Exclusivity of information] It uses a *hidden, secret, little-known* strategy recently discovered by a *private* quantitative analysis firm operating on a *non-disclosure agreement,* and that's why we keep this portfolio *under wraps,* and why this is all *behind-the-scenes* information. We don't want competitors capitalizing on this *obscure* strategy. [Exclusivity of priority] But you, as our valued client, get *first priority.* Nobody is competing with you for ownership of this portfolio; you get to *take ownership first.*"

And you can even layer on scarcity at the end there: "nobody is competing with you for ownership of this portfolio; you get to take ownership first, *but that changes in 48 hours when we roll it out to the public at large. Who knows how much it will cost then?*"

Historical Example: "Raised in unrivaled prosperity, we inherit an economy that is still the world's strongest, but is weakened by business failures, stagnant wages, increasing inequality, and deep divisions among our people. [...] Our democracy must be not only the envy of the world but the engine of our own renewal. There is nothing wrong with America that cannot be cured by what is right with America." – Bill Clinton

THE EIGHT SECONDS

How to satisfy a hidden checklist your audience evaluates you with before it's too late.

In the first eight seconds of your communication, you will either lose or win. What happens in the first eight seconds? Your audience uses micro-cues to instantly evaluate you. And remember the halo-effect: What they perceive in their first evaluation will haunt you or help you throughout the rest of your communication.

And also keep in mind the first-impression effect: We weigh our final judgement of something disproportionately by our first impression of it.

Put simply, in the first eight seconds, your audience asks themselves the following question subconsciously: "should I pay attention?"

And how do they answer that critical question? By quickly running through a checklist. And do we know what's in their checklist? We do and we don't. We don't know exactly what the checklist is. But neither do they as it occurs subconsciously. Fortunately, we do know the important parts of the checklist, based on our knowledge of human psychology.

All else equal, this is what will almost always appear on every checklist (every audience has a different one and every audience member in an audience has a different one as well): Do I find this speaker trustworthy? Do I have to use too many mental calories to take in this information? Do I have something to gain from this information? Do I have any competing inputs that might be more fruitful? Do I like this speaker? Do I think this speaker knows what I need? Do I think this speaker understands my pain points? Do I think this speaker can be the steward of a valuable solution to a problem in my life? Do I think this information will help me survive and thrive? Do I think this speaker understands me and cares about me? Do I think this speaker is self-motivated, and wants to gain something from me? Do I think there's anything in it for me? If you want some extra insight into the checklist, cede to your audience persona.

When you are speaking – meaning that you are using vocal language, body language, and verbal language – the audience applies the checklist to each of your languages. If your words are promising and pass the checklist with flying colors but the messages conveyed by your voice and body language don't, then neither do you. Not only do you have to pass the checklist, but you have to pass it with each of your languages.

DON'T MESS UP IN THE FIRST EIGHT SECONDS

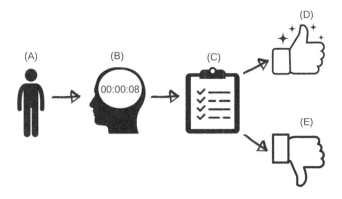

FIGURE 69: When a new speaker (A) appears to the audience, in about eight seconds (B) they run through a mental checklist (C) to decide if they approve (D) or disapprove (E); trust or distrust; like or dislike.

Historical Example: "Today we celebrate the *mystery* of American renewal." – Bill Clinton

ANCHOR THEORY

How to make any negotiation or meeting work in your favor by speaking first.

The first number a person hears will sway all future numbers even if the context of the first number has nothing to do with the context of the future numbers.

Consider a price negotiation. Imagine that the other person has been exposed to a large number that has to do with the price of an unrelated good. That very large number will, in some instances, push their consideration of a price point for the relevant good substantially higher. Why? Because the subconscious mind irrationally anchors itself to that number and runs through the mechanism of insufficient adjustment: starting at the anchor and adjusting in the appropriate direction but not adjusting far enough.

Anchor: the price of a $60,000 car on prominent display. Relevant number: the price of a care objectively valued at $20,000 in the same dealership. Insufficient adjustment: Instead of ignoring the $60,000, the mind starts at $60,000, and adjusts down from that, but doesn't adjust far enough; it only adjusts to $30,000, for example.

KEY INSIGHT:

What We Hear First Impacts How We Receive and Perceive Everything That Follows.

VISUALIZING THE ANCHORING PRINCIPLE

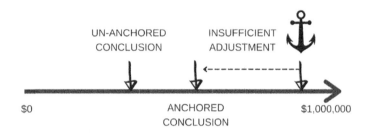

FIGURE 70: An anchor set at a high value becomes the starting point of your evaluation. You begin at the anchor and adjust from it in the appropriate direction, but do so insufficiently. In this example, this leaders to a higher anchored conclusion. Your un-anchored conclusion would have been lower. This is in favor of the "anchorer."

The impact of the anchor number can be huge, causing up to 50% adjustment in certain instances. If you are shopping online and see a crossed-out retail price that is up to ten times the price on the online store, that is an anchor. You don't adjust far enough down from that anchor, and you arrive at a price evaluation much higher than the price at the online store, which makes that price appear like a steal.

Apply unrelated anchoring: Before getting into a sales pitch, for example, talk about a very high purchase price for a good that is not directly related. Do so naturally. Don't make it so unrelated that it seems out of the blue, but don't make it so related that it seems related. Further, don't make the anchor price so unreasonably high, because if you do, the mind is more likely to resist the anchoring effect and reject that anchor as the starting point of adjustment.

Apply related anchoring. The higher retail price on the only store is an example of related anchoring. Perform related anchoring by anchoring the evaluation of your prospects and customers with the price of a directly related good.

"Other firms charge [insert higher anchor number] for products with [insert lower anchor number] of positive features." "Most products of this kind go for [insert higher anchor number]." "It used to be [higher anchor number], but we're offering you a discount of..."

Anchoring doesn't only apply to price. Any number works. Product features? Product reviews? If it's a number, it works. And anchor theory doesn't just have to do with insufficient downward adjustment from a higher anchor. You can set a lower anchor and benefit from insufficient upward adjustment too.

KEY INSIGHT:

We Will Often Stubbornly Cling to a Belief Not Because It Is the Best or Most Logical, But Simply Because It Came First.

The Older a Belief, the Greater the Risk of Our Identity Being Wrapped Up With It.

COGNITIVE-BIAS THEORY

How to immediately apply a proven theory of psychology to persuade people with ease.

When people are pondering why something happened, the explanation that is most persuasive – the one they will believe – is the one that is the most mentally available, the most coherent, the most simple, the most plausible, the most visualizable, the most fluently retrieved from memory, the most consistent with other beliefs, the most internally consistent with itself, and the most likely to appeal to group thinking.

The implication is obvious. Make your message available (availability is ease of recall – messages recalled faster are trusted and valued more). Make your message coherent. Make your message simple. Make your message plausible. Make your message visual. Make your message fluent. Make your message externally consistent. Make your message internally consistent. Make your message appeal to the values of the group.

HOW TO APPEAL TO THE PSYCHOLOGY OF TRUST

THE BIAS	APPEALING TO IT
How do you make it available?	Repeat the message in literal and figurative form.
How do you make it coherent?	Clearly explain the logical warrants (connections between the evidence and the claims).
How do you make it simple?	Use simple language and cut out unnecessary units of meaning.
How do you make it plausible?	Avoid subject-areas of high skepticism when possible.
How do you make it visual?	Support the message with compelling and visual stories.
How do you make it fluent?	Provide a memory template to your audience based on a trigger: "when [insert occurrence] happens, I want

	you to remember that [insert message]."
How do you make it externally consistent?	Mesh your message with other beliefs the audience holds by identifying the most strongly held beliefs of your audience persona and making your message the explanation of those beliefs: "[insert message] is the reason [insert belief] is true."
How do you make it internally consistent?	Avoid any inherently self-contradictory statements.
How do you make it appeal to the group-values?	Identify your message with group-based identity: "[insert group] believes [insert message] because [insert reasons]."

HOW COGNITIVE BIASES OFFER YOU INSTANT INFLUENCE

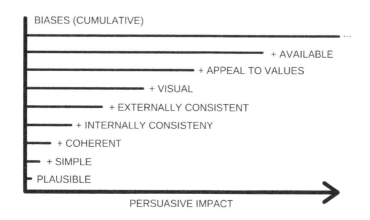

FIGURE 71: The increase in your influence that occurs as you appeal to more cognitive biases is nonlinear.

THE PEAK-END RULE

How to use a hidden secret of experiential theory that missed, might ruin your communication.

The moment of peak intensity and the end of an experience dominate someone's memory of it. And the remembering self – more so than the experiencing self – is the self that makes evaluations and judgements of a past experience.

While the mainstream formulation of this rule is as the peak-end rule, I suspect that it is more like the start-peak-end rule: People remember an experience by the start, the end, and the most intense part of the middle.

So, how do you use this in your communication? Take the key message you want people to remember and deliver it at the beginning, at the end, and at moment of peak intensity. Take the message you want people to remember, and deliver it to them at the times when people remember the things they hear.

WHAT DO PEOPLE REMEMBER? HOW DO MEMORIES FORM?

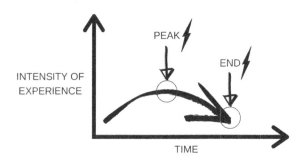

FIGURE 72: People remember the moment of peak intensity and the end.

This also applies to memory of your performance, not just your message. Are you getting evaluated, perhaps on the technicalities of your presentation delivery? Be particularly good at the beginning, the end, and the moment of peak intensity. Is your idea being evaluated? Make it seem particularly good at the beginning, the end, and the moment of peak intensity. (Of course, make your idea and delivery seem as good as possible as often as possible – this just represents another application of the theory).

WIIFM

The one question that will make your communication win or lose every single time you speak (new: implicit and explicit).

Always remember the WIIFM – or "what's in it for me?" – question and answer it in the first fifteen seconds of your communication, either implicitly or explicitly, but preferably both.

To answer the WIIFM question explicitly, you use your words to promise some sort of benefit to your audience. But you must also implicitly answer the WIIFM question: You must answer it with your subliminal languages; languages that imply things about you. And what are these subliminal languages? Your vocal language and your body language.

You must explicitly use your words to answer the WIIFM question, but you must also use your vocal delivery and body to answer the WIIFM question by implicitly imparting the words "I know what I'm talking about, I'm an expert in my field, I'm confident in this, don't waste my time and I won't waste yours, because I'm about to quickly drop a mountain of valuable information on you."

Historical Example: "For everywhere we look, there is work to be done. The state of our economy calls for action, bold and swift. And we will act, not only to create new jobs, but to lay a new foundation for growth. We will build the roads and bridges, the electric grids and digital lines that feed our commerce and bind us together. We'll restore science to its rightful place, and wield technology's wonders to raise health care's quality and lower its cost. We will harness the sun and the winds and the soil to fuel our cars and run our factories. And we will transform our schools and colleges and universities to meet the demands of a new age. All this we can do. All this we will do. Now, there are some who question the scale of our ambitions, who suggest that our system cannot tolerate too many big plans. Their memories are short, for they have forgotten what this country has already done, what free men and women can achieve when imagination is joined to common purpose, and necessity to courage. What the cynics fail to understand is that the ground has shifted beneath them, that the stale political arguments that have consumed us for so long no longer apply. The question we ask today is not whether our government is too big or too small, but whether it works – whether it helps families find jobs at a decent wage, care they can afford, a retirement that is dignified. Where the answer is yes, we intend to move forward. Where the answer is no, programs will end. And those of us who manage the public's dollars will be held to account, to spend wisely, reform bad habits, and do our business in the light of day, because only then can we restore the vital trust between a people and their government. Nor is the question before us whether the market is a force for good or ill. Its power to generate wealth and expand freedom is unmatched. But this crisis has reminded us that without a watchful eye, the market can spin out of control. The nation cannot prosper long when it favors only the prosperous. The success of our economy has always depended not just on the size of our gross domestic product, but on the reach of our prosperity, on the ability to extend opportunity to every willing heart – not out of charity, but because it is the surest route to our common good." – Barack Obama

WYSIATI

How to use the bedrock principle of human psychology to achieve guaranteed persuasion.

When evaluating the truth of a statement, people use the evidence they have without considering the quality of that evidence; without considering its bias or completeness. In *Thinking, Fast and Slow* Daniel Kahneman describes it as "what you see is all there is," or WYSIATI.

This explains why people are influenced by clearly biased individuals unless they exert great mental effort to adjust against that bias (and when they do, they will often adjust insufficiently).

Often, when evaluating the truth of your statements, the only evidence people will use is the evidence they have and that is only the evidence that you have given them.

This explains so much. This is monumental. Why does the standard persuasive communication model, of "[insert claim] is true because [insert evidence]" work? A better question is this: Why does this model work even if the claim is dubious and the evidence is incomplete? Because, what the audience sees is all there is, and all-too-often, what they see is the evidence given by the clearly biased speaker.

PACING AND LEADING

How to slowly slide people from their point of view to yours with a secret strategy of influence.

What if all you had to do to drastically improve the efficacy of your persuasion, influence, and communication, was implement one simple strategy? This is the truth when you use pacing and leading, which works with surprising reliability and lowers the tension that may arise in many scenarios (like negotiations or disagreements).

Persuasive communication is leading people to your point of view. But if you want to lead people, show them that you can match their pace first. Why? Because people have a natural aversion to being led; it's called persuasion aversion, and this one simple function of the human mind thwarts much of our persuasive communication.

So, what does this mean in a practical sense? This: Instead of getting straight into asserting your position and speaking your mind (leading), echo the sentiment of your audience's position and speak your audience's mind (pacing).

For example, let's say that your audience's position is "X is bad," and your position is "X is good." There are two ways you can go about this, and one is drastically more effective, yet sadly less common.

Leading: "X is good."

Pacing and leading: "I hear what you're saying, honestly... X has [insert bad characteristic], and [insert bad characteristic two]. It can be frustrating when X makes us feel [insert negative emotion]. Trust me, I get it. X is also [insert good characteristic one], and [insert good characteristic two]. One time, I was struggling with [insert unrelated struggle], and it was X that helped me out. All in all, X isn't so terrible. X isn't so bad. X is good."

When you psychologically assault people with an opposing point of view, they are immediately entrenched, ready for war. And make no mistake: it is psychological assault. The areas of the brain that light up during physical assault light up in an argument too.

When you start by pacing, you prevent them from jumping into their mental trenches and pulling out their cognitive disconfirmation guns. You don't trigger reactance: the human tendency to leap into motivational state that is aimed at re-establishment of a threatened or eliminated freedom (in this case, the freedom of having and voicing their own opinions). And when you slowly slide from pacing them to leading them, they don't even realize what is happening, and never have time to jump into their trenches, on the defensive. On the contrary, they feel affirmed, and people who feel affirmed are more willing to affirm. They feel open, and more receptive to your ideas, all because you showed them the same courtesy and they feel that they are heard and that their opinions are valued.

HOW TO WIN ANY ARGUMENT WITH PACING AND LEADING

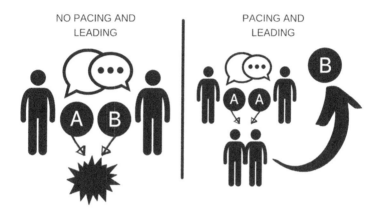

FIGURE 73: Without pacing and leading, your interlocuter says "A" and you say "B." This leads to a conflict. Conflict doesn't produce agreement. With pacing and leading, your interlocuter says "A" and you say "A." Defensiveness diminishes. You are on the same team. Then, together, you slowly, subtly, and gently slide toward "B." (I've noted two types of "arguments" – arguments in which your goal is to try to persuade the other mind, and arguments in which your goal is to try to persuade an audience. If your goal is solely to persuade an audience – a third party – conflict with the other mind – which is also trying to persuade the audience in the opposite direction – is often necessary).

Now, for the first of our pacing and leading guidelines, don't use words like "but, yet, still, though," when you shift from pacing to leading. Why? Because those words signal a discounting of what you just said: a discounting of the pacing. And that ruins it, or at the very least diminishes its impact by showing your hand. Try to slide from pacing to leading without using one of these words. It's tricky, but check out the example on the previous page. Don't worry if you use one of these discounter words: It's not the end of the world.

For the second of our guidelines, and as a testament to the value of pacing and leading, you must remember this: Pacing works even if the other person is not opposed, but neutral. If they are unsure, you can pace their uncertainty. If people are [insert any quality one] about a subject, whether it is uncertain, angry, or opposed, then you can pace that quality before leading them to [insert any quality two], whether that is certain, relaxed, or in agreement. Quality two does not have to be a converse of quality one. You can pace from any starting point and lead to any ending point.

Pacing and leading brings us to a general rule: The halo effect. How people feel about the beginning of your communication is how they are likely to feel about the end of it, even if the end contradicts the start in sentiment. And pacing and leading guarantees that they will feel good about the start, thus better about the end.

And you need to strike a balancing act. Let's say you're pacing and leading from "X is bad" to "X is good." If you pace too much, excessively affirming and reaffirming "X is bad," any leading is weakened, and the starting sentiment is strengthened. On the contrary, if you pace too little, the whole thing falls apart; leading is weakened then too, because the pacing has not yet taken effect, and the entire scheme seems disingenuous.

So, you must strike a balance: Pace enough so that it takes the effect of opening someone's mind, not so much that it takes the effect of further entrenching their original opinion; and lead enough so that it takes the effect of imparting your point of view, but not so much that its weight crumbles the whole scheme.

THE KEY TO EFFECTIVE PACING AND LEADING

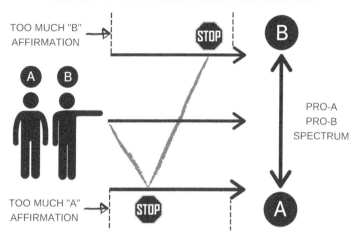

FIGURE 74: If you affirm "A" too heavily, your subsequent affirmation of "B" and the strength of the strategy at large is weakened. If you affirm "B" too heavily, the subtlety and gentleness of the strategy is lost along with its impact. Not pictured in this figure are the dangers of insufficient pacing and insufficient leading.

This previous guideline can be summarized in this sentence: Make your pacing and leading gradual, gentle, and honest. And before we move on, remember the broader wisdom of pacing and leading: If you want to prove someone wrong in such a way that he admits it, start – that doesn't mean start and continue, but start – by telling him he's right.

BENEFIT TAGGING

How to retain influence and impact throughout your communication and increase its success rate.

WIIFM doesn't just happen at the beginning of your communication, during the mental checklist phase. Here's the ongoing loop that happens in people's minds all the time: "While I am existing... will continuing this activity yield a net benefit (perceived marginal benefit > perceived marginal cost), including opportunity cost in perceived marginal benefit (the net benefit of the best forgone alternative)? If so, continue this activity. Is the opposite true? If so, stop this activity."

In other words, while you must satisfy the WIIFM question in a strong way early in your communication to get attention, you must repeatedly touch on the WIIFM question throughout your communication to keep attention.

And this raises an interesting question: *how do you do it?* How do you continuously touch upon the WIIFM question with your communication? I'm sure there are multiple ways, but one of the easiest, most effective, and most subtle ways is with benefit tagging. Benefit tagging is low cost (a tiny number of words) but massive reward (a massive amount of influence gained).

What's benefit tagging? It's simple: identify your main benefit propositions (how will your audience benefit?) and tag them throughout your communication. Boil it down to a simple, straightforward statement, like "get more sales, lose fewer clients, and make more money," and repeatedly tag this onto your communication.

For example: instead of saying "our service includes [insert feature]," say "our service includes [insert feature], to help you get more sales, lose fewer clients, and make more money." The goal is to make the core benefits your audience will receive *top of mind*, always on the cusp of their consciousness, so that everything you say will be received through the lens of "what's in it for me? *A lot, clearly.*"

And all you have to do to achieve that is repeatedly tag benefit statements throughout your speech. Two quick guidelines: they don't always have to be the same benefits, or the same benefits delivered with the same words; keep it varied to maximize the impact of benefit tagging.

THE PEOPLE'S PAIN

How to instantly gain total respect and undivided attention with one single strategy.

Remember this: People have problems that cause pain, and effective communicators speak in terms of solving these problems and easing the pain.

It's that simple. It's that easy. But it's deeply powerful. Want to become an incredibly compelling and effective communicator that changes minds, influences people, and commands total respect and undivided attention? Then all you have to do is speak in terms of the people's pain.

Go back to your audience persona. What are the problems they would love to solve? What keeps them up at night? What causes the negative emotions that bother them all day? What do they, above all, want to fix? What is the central conflict in their life that is both important and directly relevant to your subject?

Figure out the answer to these questions, and speak in terms of it. Usually, the problem will be centered around some sort of loss. Remember loss aversion? Loss produces the most extreme emotional arousal – often about twice as extreme as an equivalent gain. So, consider the people's pain from the perspective of what they might lose or have already lost. What do they get back that they've lost? This principle was certainly considered in the making of Trump's "Make America Great Again" slogan (which he borrowed from Ronald Reagan). For some reason, the pain of having something great and losing it is worse than never having something great at all. Why? Because the fall from grace is painful – because of loss aversion, and because the initially satisfied state is a type of "soft" anchor against which people compare the lacking present.

We turn to a core truth of compelling communication that connects to the benefit tagging technique. Often, the best benefit and best answer to the "WIIFM" question is not only what they will gain, but what they will not lose. Engineer your benefit statements accordingly.

Historical Example: "In such a spirit on my part and on yours we face our common difficulties. They concern, thank God, only material things. Values have shrunken to fantastic levels; taxes have risen; our ability to pay has fallen; government of all kinds is faced by serious curtailment of income; the means of exchange are frozen in the currents of trade; the withered leaves of industrial enterprise lie on every side; farmers find no markets for their produce; the savings of many years in thousands of families are gone. More important, a host of unemployed citizens face the grim problem of existence, and an equally great number toil with little return. Only a foolish optimist can deny the dark realities of the moment." – Franklin Delano Roosevelt

---

KEY INSIGHT:

Everyone Carries a Burden of Past Pain, Unlived Life, and Cynical Self-Limiting Beliefs.

The Role of a Leader Is to Replace the Self-Limiting Beliefs with Empowering Ones.

PROBLEM-SOLUTION CONSTRUCTION

How to instantly make yourself a visionary speaker who gets respect and audience action.

Want to grab audience attention in a way that is relevant and commands respect? Want to advance your agenda for improvement in the most compelling way possible? Want to change people's minds and make them voluntarily actualize your vision? Then this structure is your best friend.

The vast majority of communicators make one of two crucial mistakes. Remember: When you are speaking, the vast majority of the time you are selling (trying to get people to adopt) medicine (a solution) to an ailment (a problem).

Mistake number one: Only talking about the medicine. Why is this a mistake? Because the medicine only makes sense in the context of the problem it solves.

Mistake number two: Only talking about the ailment. Why is this a mistake? Because pontificating on the problem is useless unless you offer a solution.

So, remember this: To avoid the two most damaging communication mistakes, you must speak in terms of both problems and solutions. Through this, you will gain power, persuasion, and influence.

Enter the problem-solution construction: "Here's the problem and the negative consequences it causes. Here's the best solution and the positive benefits it offers."

Speech structures work when scrunched down to a few sentences just as they do when they form the backbone of an entire speech. They maintain a proportional impact. The problem-solution construction need not form the entirety of a speech to work. It can be two sentences: one for the problem and one for the solution. It has the same impact on a smaller scale. I call this the principle of "lengthening and shortening."

Remember: Use a special action-oriented transition when moving from the problem to the solution. And if you want to empower your transition, make it a rhetorical question.

Shortened problem-solution construction: "[Problem] Our sales processes are dramatically inefficient, losing us money every single day. [Action-oriented rhetorical question transition] So what are we going to do about this? [Solution] We can eliminate the drastic waste by focusing our prospecting efforts in the industries where we have most experience."

Lengthened problem-solution construction: "[Problem] Our sales processes are dramatically inefficient, losing us money every single day. Our people are frustrated; our employees, management, and stockholders... not to mention our other clients who are suffering because of our inefficiency. Every day we don't solve this problem, it gets worse; our stock price has been steadily bleeding for the past few months, and our candidacy for profitable mergers is weak. [Lengthened action-oriented rhetorical question transition] So what are we going to do about this? It's clear we can't let this go on if we have any interest in preserving this firm. We are all in agreement so far, I hope. The problem is clear. But how do we actually solve it? [Solution] We can eliminate drastic waste by focusing our prospecting efforts in the industries where we have the most experience. We have account-prospectors who have a track record of success in one industry working on the industry where they have a track record of failure. Why? Why not allocate our human capital more efficiently?"

Want to strengthen this? Make your solution seem easier. Raise its perceived ease. The speaker from the previous example could add this: "And this solution demands no additional spending or employment; it costs us nothing to shift people around. It will take us a day at most, and we will face no resistance from above or below. The board knows something needs to be done, and our employees will be more than happy with the change. It's an incredibly easy change that will produce a huge positive impact."

Want to strengthen this even more? Focus on the different types of problems: external, internal, and broken-justice problems.

"What?" you ask.

"Three different types of problems?"

Yes, there are three different types of problems, and they are most effective when used together.

External problems: What specific, tangible negative impacts occur in the world? What are the negative external consequences?

Internal problems: What negative impacts occur inside the audience? What are the negative emotional consequences?

Broken-justice problems: How are the previous two problems morally unjust? How is it unfair that these problems exist? How is it undeserved?

UNDERSTANDING AND USING THE THREE TYPES OF PAIN

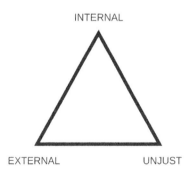

FIGURE 75: There are three different kinds of problems: external problems, internal problems, and broken-justice problems. To maximize your influence, get clarity on all three of the types of problems as they manifest themselves in your specific situation.

EXTERNAL PROBLEMS

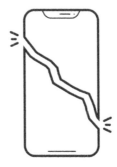

FIGURE 76: "This phone I bought immediately broke" is an external problem. It exists in the external world.

INTERNAL PROBLEMS

FIGURE 77: "I am sad because the phone I bought immediately broke" is an internal problem. It exists in the mind of the individual and an external event caused it.

BROKEN-JUSTICE PROBLEMS

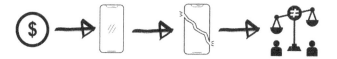

FIGURE 78: The broken-justice problem at play is that this consumer paid good money for what he was told would be a good phone but it broke immediately. This is not fair. This is unethical and represents a breach of justice.

KEY INSIGHT:

A Problem Is Something "Random" That Hurts Someone.

An Injustice Is Something with an Agent Behind It, And Something That Hurts Someone Who Doesn't Deserve It.

"[External problems] Our profitability rating is down 20%. [Internal problems] A feeling of desperation and ennui has risen within our organization, from the bottom to the top – a feeling of learned helplessness. [Broken-justice problems] It's not right that we, the firm rated most promising just last year, are now suffering and suffocating."

Historical Example: "Soldiers, Sailors, and Airmen of the Allied Expeditionary Force: You are about to embark upon the Great Crusade, toward which we have striven these many months. The eyes of the world are upon you. The hopes and prayers of liberty-loving people everywhere march with you. In company with our brave Allies and brothers-in-arms on other Fronts you will bring about the destruction of the German war machine, the elimination of Nazi tyranny over oppressed peoples of Europe, and security for ourselves in a free world. *Your task will not be an easy one. Your enemy is well trained, well equipped, and battle-hardened. He will fight savagely. But this is the year 1944. Much has happened since the Nazi triumphs of 1940-41. The United Nations have inflicted upon the Germans great defeats, in open battle, man-to-man. Our air offensive has seriously reduced their strength in the air and their capacity to wage war on the ground. Our Home Fronts have given us an overwhelming superiority in weapons and munitions of war, and placed at our disposal great reserves of trained fighting men. The tide has turned.* The free men of the world are marching together to victory. I have full confidence in your courage, devotion to duty, and skill in battle. We will accept nothing less than full victory. Good Luck! And let us all beseech the blessing of Almighty God upon this great and noble undertaking." – Dwight D. Eisenhower

MICRO-METAPHORS

How to use a secret of unforgettable eloquence to make your words sticky and memorable.

Want people to remember your words long after you've spoken them? Want to accomplish this with a proven secret of effective rhetoric used by the world's greatest communicators? This secret is micro-metaphors and micro-similes.

As the name suggests, micro-metaphors are mini-metaphors that serve to make your words more creative, compelling, and descriptive. Let me show you a sentence without them, and how we can add them in for instant and easy eloquence (typically you don't want to overload these in a single sentence, but for the sake of example...)

No micro-metaphors: "The current tax burden is hurting our economy." Identify phrases that are good candidates for metaphors: "The current *tax burden* [most nouns usually are good candidates] is *hurting* [the act of hurting something is a good candidate for a metaphor: many action-oriented phrases are good candidates] our economy [nouns are good candidates]." In other words, all of the underlined phrases are good candidates for micro-metaphors and micro-similes: "The current tax burden is hurting our economy." Attach micro-metaphors and micro-similes to the candidate phrases: "The current *ball-and-chain* of a tax burden is, *like a suffocating tsunami,* hurting the *oxygen level* of our economy."

So, what's the significance? Well, and this is just the start, the audience hears two sentences.

Sentence one: The current tax burden is hurting our economy. Sentence two: A ball and chain is suffocating our oxygen levels like a tsunami.

Remember sentiment-mapping? What do you think is (part of) the impact of micro-metaphors, if not extremely powerful sentiment mapping? Take away the preconceived notions and the sentence "the current tax burden is hurting our economy" is somewhat close to neutral in sentiment. The anti-tax-burden micro-metaphor sentence should not want to be sentiment-neutral or positive when talking about the tax burden: and thanks to the micro-metaphors, which give it a sentiment score of roughly -3, it isn't.

The micro-metaphors essentially allow you to take whatever sentiment you want to impart and intensify it. Remember the theory of degrees of intensity?

And not only do micro-metaphors create rhetorically beautiful language, with elevated bravado and intensified sentiment, but they also drive directly to the audience's subconscious mind, where they activate associative machinery.

Explicit statements always stop at the conscious filter of the receiving mind. "The tax burden is bad" will stop at that conscious filter if the audience has no preconceived notions that will waive the filter requirement.

Implicit statements, on the other hand, are not only understood, but they skip the conscious filter. So not only is the sentiment map of the anti-tax-burden sentence -3, but it is a -3 punch that is not weakened by the skeptical nature of the conscious filter (again, unless the filter is waived by a large web of preexisting beliefs, in which case it need not pass by. For example, to people who are against the tax burden, the -3 sentiment is pre-confirmed and would pass the filter anyway. But speaking cross-ideology or cross-belief system, or about a subject with no preconceived notions, the filter is active to a varying extent).

So, what do they do when they circumvent the conscious filter? What do they do when they arrive at the subconscious mind? They activate associative machinery in the subconscious. Your audience begins to associate the neutral words that are pure substance and subject with the positive or negative sentiment of the micro-metaphors.

Now, I repeat: This filter-bypassing works on neutral or moderately-agreeing audiences, but not on opposing audiences. Its efficacy on neutral audiences is enough to make it an incredibly useful tool in your communication arsenal.

Why does it not work for opposing audiences? Because their conscious filter, run by their pre-existing intellectual status quo, will be strengthened to the point of catching any opposing sentiment, even an implicit one.

And does this have any value for impromptu speeches? It depends on your skill. You can do this in impromptu speaking by thinking a phrase or sentence ahead, and then quickly moving through the three steps. Again, over time, the algorithmic three-steps become subconsciously ingrained in you and occur on their own. It may be hard at first, but it gets easy with practice. And the shocked, impressed expressions of people when they see you rattling off these vivid and compelling metaphors off the cuff is well-worth the practice.

ABOUT THIS BOOK

This book is the result of exploring a set of questions until I have uncovered enough of the answer to form a usable framework. I will briefly write about the questions and the answers, just to put this book in perspective for you.

The first question: "What makes some communication powerful, but other communication weak?" The first answer: "Among the many factors, these techniques seem to stand out in their intrinsic importance."

The second question: "Is this hypothesis supported by reality, or is the appearance misleading?" The answer: "The vast majority of world-changing, heart-moving, action-creating speeches that dominate the history textbooks used these techniques. The vast majority of communication failures did not."

The third question: "Why? What about these techniques works?" The third answer: "There are certain strategies that directly appeal to the functions of audience psychology and are inherently more effective as a result."

The fourth question: "How can I discover these techniques?" The fourth answer: "By studying the words of those who have changed the world with their communication; by identifying a technique in one of their speeches and seeking it in yet more speeches to confirm its power, and to confirm clear intent and not just coincidental arrangement of words; by identifying why that technique works, and why another technique works, and combining these two to create a third technique with its own unique persuasive power, and always by seeking the hidden secrets of world-changing persuasive communication, developing them, identifying their power, adopting them, adapting them, building upon them, stress-testing them, confirming them, denying some, and constantly discovering yet more."

So, after answering this fourth question, that's exactly what I did, and the result is what you have just read.

...............................Chapter Summary................................

- These advanced strategies are little-known secrets of influence 99% of people don't understand.
- They build upon Monroe's Motivated Sequence: Structure your message around Monroe's, sprinkle these on top.
- While Monroe's Motivated Sequence is a step-by-step process, you can use these advanced strategies *a la carte*.
- These strategies play upon the innate characteristics of human psychology, turning them to your favor.

- Some of these strategies are easier to include extemporaneously than others. Some demand preparation.
- You do not need to master every single strategy. Master a small handful, and use them well. This is sufficient.

KEY INSIGHT:

We Are Wired to Feel Deep Compassion Toward People, Not Abstractions.

We Need Stories. We Use Stories to Organize Our Minds. No Story, No Meaning. No Meaning, No Impact.

THE STRUCTURE AND THE STRATEGIES (PART TWO)

1	Monroe's Motivated Sequence
1.1	Apply Monroe's Motivated Sequence
1.2	Attention, Need, Satisfaction, Visualization, Action
1.3	Grab Attention as a Prerequisite to Influence and Persuasion
1.4	Present a Need to Validate Your Proposal or Solution
1.5	Offer the Satisfaction of the Need to Motivate Action
1.6	Present a Visualization of the Satisfaction to Raise Desire
1.7	Convey the Action that Will Move Them Toward Satisfaction
1.8	To Earn Attention, Use a Statistic
1.9	To Earn Attention, Create an Information Gap
1.10	To Earn Attention, Use "Secrecy Phrases"
1.11	To Earn Attention, Ask for a Raise of Hands
1.12	To Present a Need, Appeal to the Desire to Improve
1.13	To Present a Need, Appeal to the Life-Force Eight Core Desires
1.14	To Present a Need, Appeal to Emotion
1.15	To Present a Need, Paint a Tantalizing Image of the Future
1.16	To Offer Satisfaction, Don't Pitch Until Now
1.17	To Offer Satisfaction, Use "Safety Words"
1.18	To Offer Satisfaction, Use Personal "Safety Indicators"
1.19	To Offer Satisfaction, Apply the Rhetorical Triangle

1.20	To Create Visualization, Present Powerful Visual Adjectives
1.21	To Create Visualization, Engage the VAKOG Senses
1.22	To Create Visualization, Tap into Audience Imagination
1.23	To Create Visualization, Empower Positive Counterfactuals
1.24	To Motivate Action, Use Strong Action Verbs
1.25	To Motivate Action, Offer Tangible Takeaways
1.26	To Motivate Action, Present a Reasonable Call to Action
1.27	To Motivate Action, Tack onto Existing Habit Structures
1.28	Apply the Informational Motivated Sequence
1.29	Squish Monroe's Motivated Sequence
1.30	Place Monroe's in Front of an Informational Speech
1.31	Convey the Value of the Information and Hold Attention
2	**The Advanced Strategies**
2.1	Apply the Trifold Equation Theory of Communication
2.2	Substance = Information / Words
2.3	Sentiment = Positive Words – Negative Words
2.4	Rhetoric = (Logical + Emotional + Evidentiary) / Total Statements
2.5	Engineer Micro-Repetition for Subtle Psychological Influence
2.6	Use the PEP Model as a Micro-Structure
2.7	Use the P Quant Qual P Model for High-Level Influence

2.8	Understand the Psychology of Loss Versus Gains
2.9	Practice with the Self-Chess Strategy
2.10	Practice with the Group-Chess Strategy
2.11	Achieve Perfection and Mastery with Group Practice
2.12	Apply the Objection-Prediction Model
2.13	Reframe Commands with "Let's" Statements
2.14	Reframe Requests with "Why Don't You?" Question
2.15	Engage the Audience with The River of You
2.16	Use Open Rapport to Draw People In
2.17	Use Breaking Rapport to Achieve Authority and Credibility
2.18	Apply the Theories of Degrees of Intensity to Raise Impact
2.19	Remember the Audience Characteristic Model for Clarity
2.20	Take Advantage of the Halo Effect
2.21	Use Exclusivity Phrases to Raise the Desire For Your Proposal
2.22	Satisfy the 15-Second Checklist
2.23	Apply Anchor-Theory to Win Negotiations With Ease
2.24	Appeal to the ACSPVFCCG Elements of Psychology
2.25	Optimize Your Message for the Peak-End Rule
2.26	Answer the Critical "WIIFM?" Question
2.27	Take Advantage of the Cognitive Limitation of "WYSIATI"

2.28	Apply Pacing and Leading to Influence with Gentle Grace
2.29	Use Benefit Tagging to Retain Influence and Attention
2.30	Speak to the People's Pain to Motivate Enthusiastic Action
2.31	Use Problem-Solution Constructions for Contrast and Impact
2.32	Apply Micro-Metaphors for Subtle and Eloquent Influence

Email Peter D. Andrei, the author of the Speak for Success collection and the President of Speak Truth Well LLC directly.

pandreibusiness@gmail.com

KEY INSIGHT:

The Moment Rhetoric Starts to Stand In the Way Of Your Connection With Your Audience, Drop It. The Whole Point of Rhetoric Is To Empower That Connection.

THE ADVANCED STATEGIES LAYER ON TOP OF
MONROE'S MOTIVATED SEQUENCE

"WIIFM?"   Benefit-Tagging   Pacing Leading

+   +   +

Micro-Metaphors   Anchor Theory   PQQP and PEP

+   +   +

ATTENTION   SATISFACTION   ACTION

NEED   VISUALIZATION

+   +

Speak to Pain   Exclusivity Phrases

+   +

Micro-Repetition   Degrees of Intensity

Claim These Free Resources that Will Help You Unleash the Power of Your Words and Speak with Confidence. Visit www.speakforsuccesshub.com/toolkit for Access.

18 Free PDF Resources

12 Iron Rules for Captivating Story, 21 Speeches that Changed the World, 341-Point Influence Checklist, 143 Persuasive Cognitive Biases, 17 Ways to Think On Your Feet, 18 Lies About Speaking Well, 137 Deadly Logical Fallacies, 12 Iron Rules For Captivating Slides, 371 Words that Persuade, 63 Truths of Speaking Well, 27 Laws of Empathy, 21 Secrets of Legendary Speeches, 19 Scripts that Persuade, 12 Iron Rules For Captivating Speech, 33 Laws of Charisma, 11 Influence Formulas, 219-Point Speech-Writing Checklist, 21 Eloquence Formulas

Claim These Free Resources that Will Help You Unleash the Power of Your Words and Speak with Confidence. Visit www.speakforsuccesshub.com/toolkit for Access.

30 Free Video Lessons

We'll send you one free video lesson every day for 30 days, written and recorded by Peter D. Andrei. Days 1-10 cover authenticity, the prerequisite to confidence and persuasive power. Days 11-20 cover building self-belief and defeating communication anxiety. Days 21-30 cover how to speak with impact and influence, ensuring your words change minds instead of falling flat. Authenticity, self-belief, and impact – this course helps you master three components of confidence, turning even the most high-stakes presentations from obstacles into opportunities.

Claim These Free Resources that Will Help You Unleash the Power of Your Words and Speak with Confidence. Visit <u>www.speakforsuccesshub.com/toolkit</u> for Access.

2 Free Workbooks

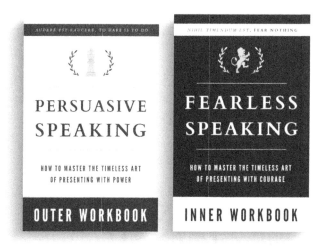

We'll send you two free workbooks, including long-lost excerpts by Dale Carnegie, the mega-bestselling author of *How to Win Friends and Influence People* (5,000,000 copies sold). *Fearless Speaking* guides you in the proven principles of mastering your inner game as a speaker. *Persuasive Speaking* guides you in the time-tested tactics of mastering your outer game by maximizing the power of your words. All of these resources complement the Speak for Success collection.

SOMETHING WAS MISSING. THIS IS IT.

D ECEMBER OF 2021, I COMPLETED the new editions of the 15 books in the Speak for Success collection, after months of work, and many 16-hour-long writing marathons. The collection is over 1,000,000 words long and includes over 1,700 handcrafted diagrams. It is *the* complete communication encyclopedia. But instead of feeling relieved and excited, I felt uneasy and anxious. Why? Well, I know now. After writing over 1,000,000 words on communication across 15 books, it slowly dawned on me that I had missed the most important set of ideas about good communication. What does it *really* mean to be a good speaker? This is my answer.

THERE ARE THREE DIMENSIONS OF SUCCESS

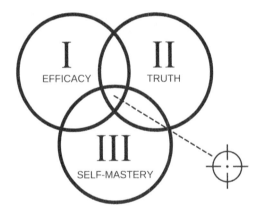

FIGURE I: A good speaker is not only rhetorically effective. They speak the truth, and they are students of self-mastery who experience peace, calm, and deep equanimity as they speak. These three domains are mutually reinforcing.

I realized I left out much about truth and self-mastery, focusing instead on the first domain. On page 33, the practical guide is devoted to domain I. On page 42, the ethical guide is devoted to domain II. We will shortly turn to domain III with an internal guide.

WHAT A GOOD SPEAKER LOOKS LIKE

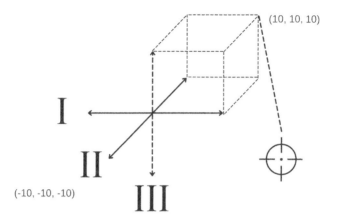

FIGURE II: We can conceptualize the three domains of success as an (X, Y, Z) coordinate plane, with each axis extending between -10 and 10. Your job is to become a (10, 10, 10). A (-10, 10, 10) speaks the truth and has attained self-mastery, but is deeply ineffective. A (10, -10, 10), speaks brilliantly and is at peace, but is somehow severely misleading others. A (10, 10, -10), speaks the truth well, but lives in an extremely negative inner state.

THE THREE AXES VIEWED DIFFERENTLY

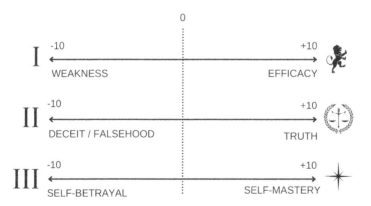

FIGURE III: We can also untangle the dimensions of improvement from representation as a coordinate plane, and instead lay them out flat, as spectrums of progress. A

(+10, -10, -10) is a true monster, eloquent but evil. A (10, 10, 10) is a Martin Luther King. A more realistic example is (4, -3, 0): This person is moderately persuasive, bends truth a little too much for comfort (but not horribly), and is mildly anxious about speaking but far from falling apart. Every speaker exists at some point along these axes.

THE EXTERNAL MASTERY PROCESS IS INTERNAL TOO

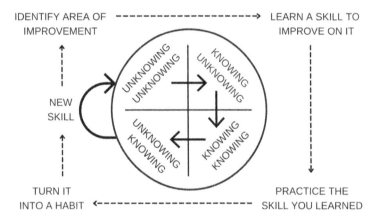

IDENTIFY AREA OF IMPROVEMENT — — — — — — — — — — — — — — → LEARN A SKILL TO IMPROVE ON IT

NEW SKILL

TURN IT INTO A HABIT ← — — — — — — — — — — — — — — — — PRACTICE THE SKILL YOU LEARNED

FIGURE IV: The same process presented earlier as a way to achieve rhetorical mastery will also help you achieve self-mastery. Just replace the word "skill" with "thought" or "thought-pattern," and the same cyclical method works.

THE THREE AXES, IN DIFFERENT WORDS

Domain One	Domain Two	Domain Three
Efficacy	Truth	Self-Mastery
Rhetoric	Research	Inner-Peace
Master of Words	Seeker of Truth	Captain of Your Soul
Aristotle's "Pathos"	Aristotle's "Logos"	Aristotle's "Ethos"
Impact	Insight	Integrity
Presence of Power	Proper Perspective	Power of Presence
Inter-Subjective	Objective	Subjective
Competency	Credibility	Character
External-Internal	External	Internal
Verbal Mastery	Subject Mastery	Mental Mastery
Behavioral	Cognitive	Emotional

THE POWER OF LANGUAGE

Language has generative power. This is why many creation stories include language as a primordial agent playing a crucial role in crafting reality. "In the beginning was the Word, and the Word was with God (John 1:1)."

Every problem we face has a story written about its future, whether explicit or implicit, conscious or subconscious. Generative language can rewrite a story that leads downward, turning it into one that aims us toward heaven, and then it can inspire us to realize this story. It can remove the cloud of ignorance from noble possibilities.

And this is good. You can orient your own future upward. That's certainly good for you. You can orient the future upward for yourself and for your family. That's better. And for your friends. That's better. And for your organization, your community, your city, and your country. That's better still. And for your enemies, and for people yet unborn; for all people, at all times, from now until the end of time.

And it doesn't get better than that.

Sound daunting? It is. It is the burden of human life. It is also the mechanism of moral progress. But start wherever you can, wherever you are. Start by acing your upcoming presentation.

But above all, remember this: all progress begins with truth.

Convey truth beautifully. And know thyself, so you can guard against your own proclivity for malevolence, and so you can strive toward self-mastery. Without self-mastery, it's hard, if not nearly impossible, to do the first part; to convey truth beautifully.

Truth, so you do good, not bad; impact, so people believe you; and self-mastery, as an essential precondition for truth and impact. Imagine what the world would be like if everyone were a triple-ten on our three axes. Imagine what good, what beauty, what bliss would define our existence. Imagine what good, what beauty, what bliss *could* define our existence, here and now.

It's up to you.

THE INNER GAME OF SPEAKING

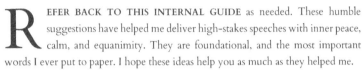

REFER BACK TO THIS INTERNAL GUIDE as needed. These humble suggestions have helped me deliver high-stakes speeches with inner peace, calm, and equanimity. They are foundational, and the most important words I ever put to paper. I hope these ideas help you as much as they helped me.

MASTER BOTH GAMES. Seek to master the outer game, but also the inner game. The self-mastery game comes before the word-mastery game, and even the world-mastery game. In fact, if you treat *any* game as a way to further your self-mastery, setting this as your "game above all games," you can never lose.

ADOPT THREE FOUNDATIONS. Humility: "The other people here probably know something I don't. They could probably teach me something. I could be overlooking something. I could be wrong. They have something to contribute" Passion: "Conveying truth accurately and convincingly is one of the most important things I'll ever do." Objectivity: "If I'm wrong, I change course. I am open to reason. I want to *be* right; I don't just want to seem right or convince others I am."

STRIVE FOR THESE SUPERLATIVES. Be the kindest, most compassionate, most honest, most attentive, most well-researched, and most confident in the room. Be the one who cares most, who most seeks to uplift others, who is most prepared, and who is most thoughtful about the reason and logic and evidence behind the claims.

START BY CULTIVATING THE HIGHEST VIRTUES IN YOURSELF: love for your audience, love for truth, humility, a deep and abiding desire to make the world a better place, the desire to both be heard and to hear, and the desire to both teach and learn. You will find peace, purpose, clarity, confidence, and persuasive power.

START BY AVOIDING THESE TEMPTING MOTIVES. Avoid the desire to "outsmart" people, to overwhelm and dominate with your rhetorical strength, to embarrass your detractors, to win on the basis of cleverness alone, and to use words to attain power for its own sake. Don't set personal victory as your goal. Strive to achieve a victory for truth. And if you discover you are wrong, change course.

LISTEN TO YOURSELF TALK. (Peterson, 2018). See if what you are saying makes you feel stronger, physically, or weaker. If it makes you feel weaker, stop saying it. Reformulate your speech until you feel the ground under you solidifying.

SPEAK FROM A PLACE OF LOVE. It beats speaking from a desire to dominate. Our motivation and purpose in persuasion must be love. It's ethical *and* effective.

LOVE YOUR ENEMIES (OR HAVE NONE). If people stand against you, do not inflame the situation with resentment or anger. It does no good, least of all for you.

AVOID THESE CORRUPTING EMOTIONS: resistance, resentment, and anger. Against them, set acceptance, forgiveness, and love for all, even your enemies.

PLACE YOUR ATTENTION HERE, NOW. Be where you are. Attend to the moment. Forget the past. Forget the future. Nothing is more important than this.

FOCUS ON YOURSELF, BUT NOW. Speaking gurus will tell you to focus solely on your audience. Yes, that works. But so does focusing on yourself, as long as you focus on yourself *now*. Let this focus root you in the present. Don't pursue a mental commentary on what you see. Instead, just watch. Here. Now. No judgment.

ACCEPT YOUR FEAR. Everyone fears something. If you fear speaking, don't fear your fear of speaking too. Don't reprimand yourself for it. Accept it. Embrace it, even. Courage isn't action without fear. Courage is action despite fear.

STARE DOWN YOUR FEAR. To diminish your fear, stare at the object of your fear (and the fear itself), the way a boxer faces off with his opponent before the fight. Hold it in your mind, signaling to your own psyche that you can face your fear.

CHIP AWAY AT YOUR FEAR. The path out of fear is to take small, voluntary steps toward what you fear. Gradual exposure dissolves fear as rain carves stone.

LET THE OUTER SHAPE THE INNER. Your thoughts impact your actions. But your actions also impact your thoughts. To control fear, seek to manage its outward manifestations, and your calm exterior will shape your interior accordingly.

KNOW THAT EGO IS THE ENEMY. Ego is a black storm cloud blocking the warm sunlight of your true self. Ego is the creation of a false self that masquerades as your true self and demands gratification (which often manifests as the destruction of something good). The allure of arrogance is the siren-song of every good speaker. With it comes pride and the pursuit of power; a placing of the outer game before the inner. Don't fall for the empty promises of ego-gratification. Humility is power.

DON'T IDENTIFY WITH YOUR POSITIONS. Don't turn your positions into your psychological possessions. Don't imbue them with a sense of self.

NOTICE TOXIC AVATARS. When person A speaks to person B, they often craft a false idea, a false avatar, of both themselves and their interlocuter: A1 and B1. So does person B: B2 and A2. The resulting communication is a dance of false avatars; A1, B1, B2, and A2 communicate, but not person A and B. A false idea of one's self speaks to a false idea of someone else, who then does the same. This may be why George Bernard Shaw said "the greatest problem in communication is the illusion that it has been accomplished." How do you avoid this dance of false avatars? This conversation between concepts but not people? Be present. Don't prematurely judge. Let go of your *sense* of self, for just a moment, so your real self can shine forth.

MINE THE RICHES OF YOUR MIND. Look for what you need within yourself; your strengths and virtues. But also acknowledge and make peace with your own capacity for malevolence. Don't zealously assume the purity of your own motives.

RISE ABOVE YOUR MIND. The ability to think critically, reason, self-analyze, and self-criticize is far more important than being able to communicate, write, and speak. Introspect before you extrospect. Do not identify as your mind, but as the awareness eternally watching your mind. Do not be in your mind, but above it.

CLEAR THE FOG FROM YOUR PSYCHE. Know what you believe. Know your failures. Know your successes. Know your weaknesses. Know your strengths. Know what you fear. Know what you seek. Know your mind. Know yourself. Know your capacity for malevolence and evil. Know your capacity for goodness and greatness. Don't hide any part of yourself from yourself. Don't even try.

KNOW YOUR LOGOS. In 500 B.C. Heraclitus defined Logos as "that universal principle which animates and rules the world." What is your Logos? Meditate on it. Sit with it. Hold it up to the light, as a jeweler does with a gem, examining all angles.

KNOW YOUR LIMITS. The more you delineate and define the actions you consider unethical, the more likely you are to resist when they seem expedient.

REMEMBER THAT EVERYTHING MATTERS. There is no insignificant job, duty, role, mission, or speech. Everything matters. Everything seeks to beat back chaos in some way and create order. A laundromat doesn't deal in clean clothes, nor a trash disposal contractor in clean streets. They deal in order. In civilization. In human dignity. Don't ignore the reservoir of meaning and mattering upon which you stand. And remember that it is there, no matter where you stand.

GIVE THE GIFT OF MEANING. The greatest gift you can give to an audience is the gift of meaning; the knowledge that they matter, that they are irreplaceable.

HONOR YOUR INHERITANCE. You are the heir to thousands of years of human moralizing. Our world is shaped by the words of long-dead philosophers, and the gifts they gave us: gems of wisdom, which strengthen us against the dread and chaos of the world. We stand atop the pillars of 4,000 years of myth and meaning. Our arguments and moral compasses are not like planks of driftwood in a raging sea, but branches nourished by an inestimably old tree. Don't forget it.

BE THE PERSON YOU WANT TO BE SEEN AS. How do you want to be seen by your audience? How can you actually be that way, rather than just seeming to be?

HAVE TRUE ETHOS. Ethos is the audience's perception that the speaker has their best interests at heart. It's your job to make sure this perception is accurate.

CHANGE PLACES WITH YOUR AUDIENCE. Put yourself in their shoes, and then be the speaker you would want to listen to, the speaker worthy of your trust.

ACT AS THOUGH THE WHOLE WORLD IS WATCHING. Or as though a newspaper will publish a record of your actions. Or as though you're writing your autobiography with every action, every word, and even every thought. (You are.)

ACT WITH AUDACIOUS HONOR. As did John McCain when he called Obama, his political opponent, "a decent family man, [and] citizen, that I just happen to have disagreements with." As did Socrates and Galileo when they refused to betray truth.

ADOPT A MECHANIC'S MENTALITY. Face your challenges the way a mechanic faces a broken engine; not drowning in emotion, but with objectivity and clarity. Identify the problem. Analyze the problem. Determine the solution. Execute the solution. If it works, celebrate. If not, repeat the cycle. This is true for both your inner and outer worlds: your fear of speaking, for example, is a specific problem with a specific fix, as are your destructive external rhetorical habits.

APPLY THE MASTERY PROCESS INTERNALLY. The four-step mastery process is not only for mastering your rhetoric, but also for striving toward internal mastery.

MARSHAL YOURSELF ALONG THE THREE AXES. To marshal means to place in proper rank or position – as in marshaling the troops – and to bring together and order in the most effective way. It is a sort of preparation. It begins with taking complete stock of what is available. Then, you order it. So, marshal yourself along three axes: the rhetorical axis (your points, arguments, rhetorical techniques, key phrases, etc.), the internal axis (your peace of mind, your internal principles, your mental climate, etc.), and the truth axis (your research, your facts, your logic, etc.).

PRACTICE ONE PUNCH 10,000 TIMES. As the martial arts adage says, "I fear not the man who practiced 10,000 punches once, but the man who practiced one punch 10,000 times." So it is with speaking skills and rhetorical techniques.

MULTIPLY YOUR PREPARATION BY TEN. Do you need to read a manuscript ten times to memorize it? Aim to read it 100 times. Do you need to research for one hour to grasp the subject of your speech? Aim to research for ten.

REMEMBER THE HIGHEST PRINCIPLE OF COMMUNICATION: the connection between speaker and audience – here, now – in this moment, in this place.

KNOW THERE'S NO SUCH THING AS A "SPEECH." All good communication is just conversation, with varying degrees of formality heaped on top. It's all just connection between consciousnesses. Every "difference" is merely superficial.

SEE YOURSELF IN OTHERS. What are you, truly? Rene Descartes came close to an answer in 1637, when he said "cogito, ego sum," I think therefore I am. The answer this seems to suggest is that your thoughts are most truly you. But your thoughts (and your character) change all the time. Something that never changes, arguably even during deep sleep, is awareness. Awareness is also the precondition for thought. A computer performs operations on information, but we don't say the computer "thinks." Why? Because it lacks awareness. So, I believe what makes you "you," most fundamentally, is your awareness, your consciousness. And if you accept this claim – which is by no means a mystical or religious one – then you must also see yourself in others. Because while the contents of everyone's consciousness is different, the consciousness itself is identical. How could it be otherwise?

FORGIVE. Yourself. Your mistakes. Your detractors. The past. The future. All.

FREE YOUR MIND. Many of the most challenging obstacles we face are thoughts living in our own minds. Identify these thoughts, and treat them like weeds in a garden. Restore the pristine poise of your mind, and return to equanimity.

LET. Let what has been be and what will be be. Most importantly, let what is be what is. Work to do what good you can do, and accept the outcome.

FLOW. Wikipedia defines a flow state as such: "a flow state, also known colloquially as being in the zone, is the mental state in which a person performing some activity is fully immersed in a feeling of energized focus, full involvement, and enjoyment in the process of the activity. In essence, flow is characterized by the complete absorption in what one does, and a resulting transformation in one's sense of time." Speaking in a flow state transports you and your audience outside of space and time. When I entered deep flow states during my speeches and debates, audience members would tell me that "it felt like time stopped." It felt that way for me too. Speaking in a flow state is a form of meditation. And it both leads to and results from these guidelines. Adhering to them leads to flow, and flow helps you adhere to them.

MEDITATE. Meditation brings your attention to the "here and now." It creates flow. Practice silence meditation, sitting in still silence and focusing on the motions of your mind, but knowing yourself as the entity watching the mind, not the mind itself. Practice aiming meditation, centering your noble aim in your mind, and focusing on the resulting feelings. (Also, speaking in flow is its own meditation).

EMBARK ON THE GRAND ADVENTURE. Take a place wherever you are. Develop influence and impact. Improve your status. Take on responsibility. Develop capacity and ability. Do scary things. Dare to leap into a high-stakes speech with no preparation if you must. Dare to trust your instincts. Dare to strive. Dare to lead. Dare to speak the truth freely, no matter how brutal it is. Be bold. Risk failure. Throw out your notes. The greatest human actions – those that capture our hearts and minds – occur on the border between chaos and order, where someone is daring to act and taking a chance when they know they could fall off the tightrope with no net below. Training wheels kill the sense of adventure. Use them if you need to, but only to lose them as soon as you can. Speak from the heart and trust yourself. Put yourself out there. Let people see the gears turning in your mind, let them see you grappling with your message in real time, taking an exploration in the moment. This is not an automaton doing a routine. It's not robotic or mechanical. That's too much order. It's also not unstructured nonsense. That's too much chaos. There is a risk of failure, mitigated not by training wheels, but by preparation. It is not a perfectly practiced routine, but someone pushing themselves just beyond their comfort zone, right at the cutting-edge of what they are capable of. It's not prescriptive. It's not safe either. The possibility that you could falter and fall in real-time calls out the best from you, and is gripping for the audience. It is also a thrilling adventure. Have faith in yourself, faith that you will say the right words when you need to. Don't think ahead, or backward. Simply experience the moment.

BREAK THE SEVEN LAWS OF WEAKNESS. If your goal is weakness, follow these rules. Seek to control what you can't control. Seek praise and admiration from others. Bend the truth to achieve your goals. Treat people as instruments in your game. Only commit to outer goals, not inner goals. Seek power for its own sake. Let anger and dissatisfaction fuel you in your pursuits, and pursue them frantically.

FAIL. Losses lead to lessons. Lessons lead to wins. If there's no chance of failure in your present task, you aren't challenging yourself. And if you aren't challenging yourself, you aren't growing. And that's the deepest and most enduring failure.

DON'T BETRAY YOURSELF. To know the truth and not say the truth is to betray the truth and to betray yourself. To know the truth, seek the truth, love the truth, and to speak the truth and speak it well, with poise and precision and power… this is to honor the truth, and to honor yourself. The choice is yours.

FOLLOW YOUR INNER LIGHT. As the Roman emperor and stoic philosopher Marcus Aurelius wrote in his private journal, "If thou findest in human life anything better than justice, truth, temperance, fortitude, and, in a word, anything better than thy own mind's self-satisfaction in the things which it enables thee to do according to right reason, and in the condition that is assigned to thee without thy own choice; if, I say, thou seest anything better than this, turn to it with all thy soul, and enjoy that which thou hast found to be the best. But if nothing appears to be better than [this], give place to nothing else." And as Kant said, treat humans as ends, not means.

JUDGE THEIR JUDGMENT. People *are* thinking of you. They *are* judging you. But what is their judgment to you? Nothing. (Compared to your self-judgment).

BREAK LESSER RULES IN THE NAME OF HIGHER RULES. Our values and moral priorities nest in a hierarchy, where they exist in relation to one another. Some are more important than others. If life compels a tradeoff between two moral principles, as it often does, this means there is a right choice. Let go the lesser of the two.

DON'T AVOID CONFLICT. Necessary conflict avoided is an impending conflict exacerbated. Slay the hydra when it has two heads, not twenty.

SEE THE WHOLE BOARD. Become wise in the ways of the world, and learned in the games of power and privilege people have been playing for tens of thousands of years. See the status-struggles and dominance-shuffling around you. See the chess board. But then opt to play a different game; a more noble game. The game of self-mastery. The game that transcends all other games. The worthiest game.

SERVE SOMETHING. Everyone has a master. Everyone serves something. Freedom is not the absence of service. Freedom is the ability to choose your service. What, to you, is worth serving? With your work and with your words?

TAKE RESPONSIBILITY FOR YOUR RIPPLE EFFECT. If you interact with 1,000 people, and they each interact with 1,000 more who also do the same, you are three degrees away from one billion people. Remember that compassion is contagious.

ONLY SPEAK WHEN YOUR WORDS ARE BETTER THAN SILENCE. And only write when your words are better than a blank page.

KNOW THERE IS THAT WHICH YOU DON'T KNOW YOU DON'T KNOW. Of course, there's that you know you don't know too. Recognize the existence of both of these domains of knowledge, which are inaccessible to you in your present state.

REMEMBER THAT AS WITHIN, SO (IT APPEARS) WITHOUT. If you orient your aim toward goals fueled by emotions like insecurity, jealousy, or vengeance, the world manifests itself as a difficult warzone. If you orient your aim toward goals fueled by emotions like universal compassion and positive ambition, the beneficence of the world manifests itself to you. Your aim and your values alter your perception.

ORIENT YOUR AIM PROPERLY. Actions flow from thought. Actions flow from *motives*. If you orient your aim properly – if you aim at the greatest good for the greatest number, at acting forthrightly and honorably – then this motive will fuel right actions, subconsciously, automatically, and without any forethought.

STOP TRYING TO USE SPEECH TO GET WHAT YOU WANT. Try to articulate what you believe to be true as carefully as possible, and then accept the outcome.

LEARN THE MEANING OF WHAT YOU SAY. Don't assume you already know.

USE THE MOST POWERFUL "RHETORICAL" TACTIC. There is no rhetorical tool more powerful than the overwhelming moral force of the unvarnished truth.

INJECT YOUR EXPERIENCE INTO YOUR SPEECH. Speak of what you know and testify of what you have seen. Attach your philosophizing and persuading and arguing to something real, some story you lived through, something you've seen.

DETACH FROM OUTCOME. As Stoic philosopher Epictetus said: "There is only one way to happiness and that is to cease worrying about things which are beyond the power of our will. Make the best use of what is in your power, and take the rest as it happens. The essence of philosophy is that a man should so live that his happiness shall depend as little as possible on external things. Remember to conduct yourself in life as if at a banquet. As something being passed around comes to you, reach out your hand and take a moderate helping. Does it pass you? Don't stop it. It hasn't yet come? Don't burn in desire for it, but wait until it arrives in front of you."

FOCUS ON WHAT YOU CONTROL. As Epictetus said, "It's not what happens to you, but how you react to it that matters. You may be always victorious if you will never enter into any contest where the issue does not wholly depend upon yourself. Some things are in our control and others not. Things in our control are opinion, pursuit, desire, aversion, and, in a word, whatever are our own actions. Things not in our control are body, property, reputation, command, and, in one word, whatever are not our own actions. Men are disturbed not by things, but by the view which they take of them. God has entrusted me with myself. Do not with that all things will go well with you, but that you will go well with all things." Before a high-stakes speech or event, I always tell myself this: "All I want from this, all I aim at, is to conduct what I control, my thoughts and actions, to the best of my ability. Any external benefit I earn is merely a bonus."

VIEW YOURSELF AS A VESSEL. Conduct yourself as something through which truth, brilliantly articulated, flows into the world; not as a self-serving entity, but a conduit for something higher. Speak not for your glory, but for the glory of good.

Want to Talk? Email Me:

PANDREIBUSINESS@GMAIL.COM

This is My Personal Email.
I Read Every Message and
Respond in Under 12 Hours.

Made in the USA
Las Vegas, NV
15 December 2023